THE GEN Z ANSWER KEY FOR BUSINESS

THE GO-TO GUIDE FOR MARKETING TO GENERATION Z

Sky Rota

For information contact:
Sky@GenZinsider.com/www.GenZinsider.com

Book layout and cover design by BookFuel

ISBN: 978-1-0797-4431-6

First Edition: 2017

"We must constantly look at things in a different way. Just when you think you know something, you must look at it in a different way. Even though it may seem silly or wrong, you must try. Dare to strike out and find new ground."

— *The Dead Poet's Society*

Table of Contents

Why I Wrote This Book

"Focus on your strengths, hire for your weaknesses."
—Sky Rota

The "Answer Key" in this book's title says it all.

Answer keys are where you get the answers. First of all: I'm thirteen years old, I'm in seventh grade, and when I take a test, I want the answers. I don't care who gives them to me, or what form they show up in.

That's why I don't want to add any filler to this book; I just want to tell you the answers the way I see them. Because of this, this book may feed you information more quickly than you are accustomed to.

Generation Z is proving that we are somewhat of an old-soul generation; some of us are way more mature than our age suggests. We started at a young age because technology was available to us from birth. Maturity and adulthood don't come with a number. (My mother says sometimes they never come.) The flip side of this is that just being an adult doesn't make you more advanced in a topic, especially a topic like how to market to Generation Z.

Patience does usually come when you are older; I don't have patience and I like instant gratification. That's why I am giving you the real version from my point of view, the way I see things. As you have read in many business books before, no one really has all the answers. I created this book because I felt the need to share my knowledge with the rest of the world. I'm trying to help make it a better place. I come from an entrepreneurial family, so I want to see businesses thrive. And I want to get things right with my generation because we are the future. We are a tough generation to understand; you're going to need help. If I can offer even the tiniest bit of assistance, I'm going to give 100%. That's what I do; I help people. With my insight comes a responsibility to try my best to pass on my knowledge to brands and businesses. To educate them and to make sure you don't take as long to get to know us as you did Millennials.

I'm not going to lie to you and tell you you have an easy journey ahead of you. It's going to be hard, and you're going to be making more changes than you're used to. But you will get the hang of it; you will get to know us.

It's time to start drafting for your Generation Z team. It's time to start thinking outside the box, to start hiring people that don't look like you or act like you—and please, don't let your HR people do all the reviewing of your applications. (I'll explain later.)

Now, I need you to know I don't consider myself a writer. I'm not entering any "young authors" competition, I'm not trying to be a professional writer when I grow up, and I certainly do not physically write most things down.

I have ideas and inside information about my generation. I see what is needed and missing in my everyday life. I am constantly daydreaming, researching, making business plans, thinking of inventions, and a million other things. And despite being the baby of four kids, I live a pretty grown-up life. I spend a ton of time with adults, and my mother values my opinion and likes to hear my thoughts on most issues.

I live something of a luxury lifestyle, which gives me lots of firsthand insight into and knowledge of luxury-lifestyle experiences, and I come from an entrepreneurial background. Both of my parents had entrepreneurial fathers, so they both knew how to work and could run their family businesses from a young age. That said, although my father is a very successful businessman, I have always had a strong desire to become independently successful.

I don't want to ride on my dad's success. I want to create my own worth. Even as I'm writing this book my father has no idea that I have my new website GenZinsider.com up and running. I want to be responsible for my own accomplishments. I want to do it on my own, be my own boss, have my own companies, make my own mark on this world.

I have seen a lot, and had lots of different experiences, for a kid my age.

We all have life stories; they are just different. I've had good and bad just like everyone else. The difference is, I like to share my stories. I like to ask questions and I love to help others. I have a different perception of things that I know comes from being dyslexic. It's like a special power I have that I wouldn't give up for the world.

I didn't always feel this way about being dyslexic. I thought it was easier to be like everyone else, because life is too hard when you are different. I didn't feel like I fit in in this world because I can't learn like most people on the planet. But once I found a place where I fit in, a place that knew how to teach people like me, that was when I knew being different was a gift.

I see things most people don't see. Since I was two I've had a photographic memory. And one of the greatest gifts I possess is having exceptional empathy; it enables me to see and understand things from a completely different perspective. I have the ability to read people and see the big picture. I am an out-of-the-box thinker and have my own original insights. I'm a fighter and giving up isn't in my vocabulary.

So when reading this book, don't think about the age of the person who wrote it.

Instead, just imagine that someone handed you the Answer Key. Because in the end, it really doesn't matter where you got the answers from.

I understand that it isn't exactly regular practice for CEOs, or anyone on the corporate ladder, to turn to a kid for this invaluable info. At the same time, I bet if I put this book out without mentioning my age or showing my picture, you wouldn't think twice about using my answer key.

If you were to ask, "How can someone so young know this amount of information?" Well, I'll tell you, it wouldn't be the first time someone brought up my age. Companies have emailed me back numerous times saying I won the prize for being the youngest person to ever pitch them an idea. I'm fine with that.

Keep in mind: you are living in my world. I am a pro at it. You guys are the newcomers. We need to teach you how we operate.

If it's easier, consider this book a manual for your next generation of consumers, since back in your day everything came with a manual for how to operate it.

Do you realize that none of the devices we buy today come with a manual? Do you know why that has changed? It's not because the entire world has become dyslexic like me.

It's because we are a hands-on generation, and we figure it out on our own—or, better yet, we look up what the new product features or what the update has in store for us.

We are constantly learning, and our biggest teachers, besides ourselves, are our friends. We all share the newest features on our tech devices. We teach each other how to get that crazy emoji or what shortcut opens our camera. We constantly connect with others to learn from each other. There are reviews and message boards online to find out anything and everything you need to know. For every question you encounter, others have had the same issue before you did, and they gave back by sharing their information for others to learn from their problem.

That's what I'm doing: I'm sharing my insider information. Does that show you what a sharing generation we are?

If your CEO or head of the company is in any way like my dad, you may as well lock the doors now. (Just kidding.)

But seriously, what if you know more than your boss about the generation that supports their company/business?

See, one of the main reasons I created this Answer Key is my close-minded behind-the-times Baby-Boomer dad.

Yes, he became open to emailing back in the day, but that seems to have been the extent of his interest in anything social media related. He does not want to engage in social media in either his personal life or his business. He is not willing to educate himself about it. He doesn't even carry a cell phone on a regular basis.

So how can someone who works for him convince him how important social media is to our generation, let alone that Gen-Zers live in a totally mobile-driven society?

It's virtually impossible. He thinks we "play" on cell phones. In fact, I have been making YouTube videos for years and my dad doesn't even watch them. He hasn't even subscribed to my YouTube channels!

Now, I'm sure he is not the only businessman out there that isn't up on the importance of their company having an Instagram account, YouTube videos, and a mobile version of their website. Who owns most businesses? Old men. Not exactly the right people to learn how to market to Gen Z.

Lots of older-generation business owners don't like to try new things, and social media is as foreign as Mandarin to them. Change is difficult for them because it was not something they practiced when they were younger. Back in the day they kept things the same for twenty-five years at a time, and it worked for them. So imagine how irrational our generation appears to them, as we are constantly changing, updating, and creating new things.

True story: my father has the first iPad that came out. And he received it under protest. What's more, he's vowed to never update it.

Why, you may ask?

Because, he says, he likes that version of Scrabble and he isn't interested in it changing in any way. All of his kids have told him that the new version has this great new feature, etc. He says, "I'm not interested! I don't like change; the version I have works just fine."

You have to find someone in the company that is open-minded and comfortable with the idea of trying something new.

That is how I get a lot of my consulting jobs; someone in the company thought it was a cool idea to have this thirteen-year-old kid tell them what they were missing on their website. No one had ever before pointed out that they needed a mobile version, or told them what they were doing wrong with their social media posts, or showed them how adding an Instagram widget to their site could get them three hundred thousand followers seeing daily images of their remarkable stock items.

When you work with people in the generation you are marketing to, we can help you to see important aspects of your business that you didn't recognize.

We don't miss a thing, and we know what we want. You don't need to have years and years of experience to be an expert.

By involving Generation-Zers in your social media or marketing plans and strategies, you will get firsthand insight from the natives to whom you are trying to market! Newer businesses are hiring not just business majors to do their marketing but also sociologists/psychologists, because they want to know how the target audience thinks.

When I speak to different departments at companies, the first thing I ask is, "Do you have any staff/employees within these demographics? Why don't we ask them what they think of this strategy/plan/idea?" In every case, the company hadn't thought of their in-house people as part of the demographics they were marketing to.

Why not?

The way I see it, they have the answers right under their noses, but it's all in untapped resources.

Start involving your own people! Ask them what their thoughts and opinions are. They are not only your employees but also, virtually, your marketing demographic.

I am constantly recruiting new team members. The more input the better. I ask question and listen to their ideas. I watch behaviors everywhere I go and learn from them. Generation Z is full of everyday influencers.

Start recruiting your own people to be your ambassadors—just as, for example, I am an ambassador for my school. Because who can sell my school better than I can? Should my school hire a marketing professional to guide parent/student tours, or is it better to receive a tour straight from the source? I know the inside information. I know exactly how my school operates, because I spend five days a week there. I am the voice representing my school on those tours.

This system is very successful. All our visitors seem to feel comfort seeing a student representing the school they may potentially send their child to. They feel much more relaxed, asking me questions I know they would never feel comfortable asking an admissions director, for fear of being judged. They know that I represent the demographic of the students who will be applying, so I am the best representative to the potential applicants, and the best advocate for my school.

The lesson? It doesn't matter where your company or brand's expertise comes from, as long as the end result gets you to your goal.

Introduction

My name is Sky. I'm thirteen years old and I live in a multigenerational family. That means we are made up of a few different generations, all living in the same household. (By the way, not an easy thing.) Years ago, everyone you were marketing to consumed information the same way. But today you have to market to multiple generations at a time—for example, print ads for the Baby Boomers, email for the Gen-Xers and Millennials, and YouTube, Instagram, and even Snapchat for the Gen-Zers.

Let me tell you a little bit about us and the way we grew up to help you understand how Generation Z is so different from the ones that came before it.

I consider Generation Z to range from those born in 1993 to those born in 2010. It starts with my brother's age group—he was born in 1993 and is currently twenty-two years old. Ever since my brother was old enough to answer the classic "What do you want to be when you grow up?" question, he would say, "I want to make a difference." Before that, our parents had never even heard those words from an adult, let alone a child.

We didn't know what that difference was and we still don't, but he is currently attending the American University Washington College of Law and is completing a dual degree, a JD in law and an MA in international affairs. His path is a far cry from my entrepreneurial business-owning parents', which is pretty typical of the kids in Gen Z.

I also have two sisters, who are identical twins. They are twenty-one and in their junior year of college. They attend the same college and share a dorm room—it's a twin thing. One sister is a business/web-design/entrepreneurial-something, and the other is a psychology major. Both are soon to be nursing students, as they recently decided to become nurse practitioners. They are becoming more career-focused.

My father is fifty-nine years old and a total Baby Boomer, one of those long-haired hippies. He hitchhiked! If you have even heard that word before, you are showing your age. If you actually *were* a hitchhiker, then I am really impressed you bought my book.

My mom, on the other hand, is a Generation Xer. Her generation was pushed out the door early and had to grow up fast. This made them much more mature and worldly than our generation. They were an independent generation and went to work young. No child labor laws for them!

Because of the ways they grew up, every generation deals with technology differently.

Both my parents grew up in a world that was the opposite of "stranger danger." They trusted everyone and even got in cars with them. They walked home from school for lunch. They left the doors to their houses unlocked and played with their friends outside. No texting first to plan, or connecting through social media. They just found each other or ran into one another.

In fact there was no such thing as play dates—they actually weren't allowed inside! All playing was done outdoors. They played until it got dark out and then came in. No one called or texted them to come home. There was no means of contact between parents and their children, and they didn't need it. There was no reason to contact their parents for rides, because they weren't getting any rides. They didn't get picked up from school or swim-team practice or baseball or softball or the movies or anything else. They rode their bikes or walked.

They did have house phones, which today we call landlines. I haven't had one in my house for years, because no one was using it except the telemarketers who called to harass us. My dad did say he talked to girls on the phone every night…not sure he's telling the truth there.

So my father, like a lot of Baby Boomers, really can't stand any of our tech life today. He especially hates us using our cell phones all the time, and not for talking. He doesn't get texting one bit—"Why don't you just call your friend!" he will say.

He was actually born at almost exactly the same time as Bill Gates and Steve Jobs, and in one big way he is exactly like those two guys—he was at the forefront of the Internet startup.

My father is brilliant. He isn't a programmer or developer, but rather a serial entrepreneur and a completely different thinker, one of the crazy ones, the rebels. I mean that in the most loving way. He is one of the smart ones who saw the opportunity the Internet presented and how big it was going to be. He started buying up domain names—maybe not all the best ones, but there were quite a few home runs. His company builds software and is something of a mom-and-pop shop in Philadelphia. It's not quite Silicon Valley, but great things come in small packages.

So he did take to computers easily, but I have to remind myself that that was a few decades ago. Now he is old and can't wrap his head around the fact that I'm not just talking to one friend; I could be on a group chat with my entire class, or with just a few friends, or with ten different people at a time, including my mother popping up as well.

He doesn't like phones at the table or anywhere near him. "Put your phone down and let's talk," he will say to me while at a restaurant waiting for our food to come. "What could you possibly be playing?"

He receives every business journal known to mankind, and gets all his information from reading tangible books, magazines, newspapers—anything in written form. He is all about writing notes on paper. Meanwhile the rest of the world is trying to go paperless, but my dad actually pays more to receive our house bills in paper form. He refuses online versions of anything; he must have the tangible version in his hands. "There's something to be said about holding a newspaper," he says.

Yeah…that it's rude when you spread it out across people sitting next to you on an airplane and they have to duck out of the way!

However, he does pay for ad blockers for the auction sites and other sites he uses, as he cannot stand seeing ads pop up! He would rather pay not to ever see any. He actually works on his computer just about eighteen hours a day, emailing, bidding in auctions, and researching. He doesn't play video games, watch shows or videos, or use a cell phone, even to send texts. In fact he texts us from his email, and has no idea why we all hate it *so* much—it's like blind texting. There is no train of texts; he will email-text us and when we reply he has zero idea of what we are replying to. It is *so* frustrating. He is the email king, while we consider email today's snail mail!

Another thing: my dad doesn't have an ATM card and carries cash, which is pretty much unheard of. No one has money on them today, and he wonders why I can't really understand change. Part of it is my dyslexia, and part is because I never, ever use tangible money for anything.

While in some ways my mom's generation had a similar upbringing, they've adapted a little better to technology because they were still young when a lot of it was being invented. My mom's family in particular got everything as it came out. Their family was the first out of her friends' families to have a microwave oven, years before everyone else. She says her mother refused to use it and would only use the stove for years, and her friends were afraid of it and wouldn't stand in front of it. A few of them weren't even allowed to come over anymore once their parents found out they had a microwave in their house…lol.

They were also the first kids to have a Betamax recorder/player, which was like an early version of a VCR that cost thousands of dollars (probably equal to twelve thousand dollars in today's money). Their friends and family members were amazed that you could record a show to watch later (there was nowhere to get a movie, so they could only tape shows at this time). The videotapes were crazy expensive and only came in thirty or sixty minutes.

When my mom and her siblings were young, my grandmother gave them one hour of TV time per day to play games or watch television. She was anti all technology. Instead, she was all about reading books and newspapers, and she purchased the 1978 *World Book Encyclopedia* set for the house so she didn't have to drive them to the library to do every school report or project.

In my mother's young teen years, in the '80s, technology played a bigger role. That was the start of MTV and BET, and of music videos. Then there was *Atari*. My mom and her brother received it for Christmas as soon as it was released. There was no gender-specific stuff then; boys and girls both played video games. End of story. They came home from school every day excited to play *Space Invaders*.

So my mother is much more open to and accepting of today's technology than others of her generation, and especially more than my father's generation. She thinks it makes her life so easy and welcomes this digital age. She loves being able to simultaneously text her three college kids, her sister, and her friend all at once without having to sit on the phone and talk all night. She loves to Google and is an expert researcher. I swear she spends hours a day researching anything and everything. My mother tells us her very favorite thing in the world is her iPad Pro! Sometimes I think she loves that more than us. She says it's the greatest invention ever made and better than any gift she has ever received. I know she stays up all night watching series on Netflix and Xfinity under her covers so the light won't wake my dad. She says there is no time to sleep—too much to do between researching, watching series, or filling an Amazon cart to have shipped to one of my siblings at college.

Still, my mom is the exception. Generation Z is like light years away from my parents' time.

I sometimes feel like my parents were born hundreds of years ago. My mother tells me she is only forty-nine, not a hundred and fifty! But as far as lifestyles, she may as well be. We've had opposite lives. To our eyes, they lived in a caveman world.

It's more like they landed on our planet, instead of us landing on their planet. We are the natives, and I'm here to teach you how to talk to us.

Gen Z Basics

I'M HERE TO GIVE YOU an inside look into my generation through my eyes. You may not think Generation Z is your current market, but we have much more influencing power over our parents than ever before. Gen-Zers are the educators in our households. We keep our parents up to speed on everything that is trending.

Generation Zers speak a different language and live a lifestyle that is foreign to all generations before us. It's time you learned our language and I'm here to translate for you.

First of all, mobile is everything for us.

Gen-Zers don't care about TV, or even computers, really. Our device of choice for all content is our phone. We watch everything from truTV to YouTube to Netflix on our phones. We don't care about the size of the screen; we just want the convenience of being able to be engaged and entertained wherever we want.

If you see a younger Gen-Z kid watching something on their cell, it looks as if they only just received it today; that's how completely absorbed in the experience they are. There is no such thing as downtime or boredom today. If anything, this generation isn't getting nearly enough sleep, as there is too much going on to want to sleep and miss something. Mobile is everything to Gen-Zers. It is the only device we need in our lives.

We are the clicking, swiping, posting, following, and sharing generation.

We are the ones you say have an eight-second attention span—well, it's even less than that (about six seconds tops). We want instantaneous results and answers.

But it isn't just about our short attention spans; we have the best content-filtering abilities of all prior generations. We basically have no patience because we don't like wasting our valuable time. This is an important point to note for marketing to us.

We are the ones who never had a landline; we've never answered a phone where the person was trying to contact someone besides us. In fact, we don't even speak on phones; we text or FaceTime and are used to having live, real-time conversations. We connect through video, even if it's just watching each other talk through FaceTime while in a pool or in our bedrooms. The point is, this way of interactive talking keeps us interested; we are bored by plain old-fashioned phone calls. We want to share our interests and experiences with each other in real time.

A lot of Gen-Zers know what we want, and nothing and no one is going to hold us back from going after it.

We are confident, multi-talented, and problem-solving. We go to YouTube or other video platforms for tutorials to troubleshoot before asking for help. We are also creative, out-of-the-box thinkers that will come up with multiple solutions for any problem.

Additionally, Gen-Zers are not afraid to share our findings and give feedback to anyone. We are here to make a difference, and to this end we have learned to use our strengths to guide us and to hire for our weaknesses.

We are open-minded and used to change. We wake up to weekly updates on our devices, sometimes even daily updates.

Our lives revolve around reviews, replies, comments, and feedback. But while we are followers and sharers, we only follow those we choose to, and block all others. We don't do likes and post for just anyone to see us. We like our privacy and have learned from the previous generation, who got bit in the butt by posting things your grandmother shouldn't see. They got fired, passed over by colleges, and in much more trouble in some cases. We learned from their lessons. We share only with whom we select and prefer pics to not stick around for too long.

We are experts at accepting diversity: we don't see color, and we are used to same-gender parents, an African-American president, and transgender kids in our classrooms. We are non-judgmental and do not want to be judged by others.

We are not fazed by lock-down drills at school or by kids who learn differently.

We are not the first kids on the planet with ADHD, but we are the most diagnosed and least ashamed that we have it. Lots of us do have anxiety, OCD, and stress, but we are aware, open, and unafraid to share our issues with others. We are learning to embrace our differences and not be ashamed of them. Most

Gen-Zers have spoken to a counselor, therapist, or psychiatrist regarding one or more of our issues.

We still can't stand bullies.

We are on the quiet side and are not gossipers. We don't do drama; we want peace. We are learning what mindfulness is, and watch Ted Talks like "All it Takes is 10 Mindful Minutes," by Andy Puddicombe, to help us with our anxiety and stress.

It may be difficult for other generations to understand, but we feel a connection with our social media celebrities. They are not stars to us. They are regular people. They are real and relatable. They are sharing their experiences, their lives, with us through their videos, whether of a prank, washing their dog, getting engaged, or describing their wisdom-teeth removal. They are truthful and let us into their lives. We know their families, parents, pets, and the friends they hang out with. We listen, hear them, and care. They keep entertainment interesting and only give us bite-sized content. They know us and hold our short attention span. They know how we need to be entertained, and they provide us with constant new content—no reruns for Gen-Zers.

If these YouTube influencers taught school, no one would need an IEP (an Individual Education Plan for students with various learning needs). They would keep us engaged because they know we are all visual learners in this generation, which is why regular school doesn't work for us. School is moving too slowly for our minds today. There is a reason that the number of schoolchildren with IEPs is rapidly growing (according to the National Center for Education Statistics, the national average is over twelve percent of students). School has never changed and gotten with the times. (But that's another story...)

Social media celebs share with us and teach us to be real. The "nerds" who play video games are crazy popular, and gaming is considered a sport. They remind us that all that matters in life is to be true to yourself and embrace your differences and talents. We understand that not everyone is going to love you and be your friend, and we can live with that.

Compare us to the previous generation:

Millennials had friends; Gen-Zers have followers.

Millennials had likes; Gen-Zers have shares.

Millennials posted risky pics; Gen-Zers post safe pics.

Millennials loved to text; Gen-Zers love to FaceTime.

Millennials tweeted their lives; Gen-Zers tweet for business.

Millennials had their own websites; Gen-Zers have their own YouTube channels.

Millennials had contacts; Gen-Zers have followings.

Millennials loved Facebook; Gen-Zers love SnapChat.

Millennials were bloggers; Gen-Zers are vloggers.

Millennials had American Idol; Gen-Zers have America's Got Talent.

Millennials Googled; Gen-Zers YouTube.

Millennials binge-watched series; Gen-Zers binge-watch YouTube.

Millennials watched TV (on a television); Gen-Zers stream content on phones.

Millennials had the Kardashians; Gen-Zers have YouTube pranksters.

Millennials were friends with their parents; Gen-Zers unfollow their parents.

Millennials liked content; Gen-Zers like bullet points.

Millennials liked to go shopping; Gen-Zers like to shop online

Millennials used Tinder; Gen-Zers meet face to face.

How Gen-Zers Interact With the World

I'M GOING TO START OUT by telling you an example that displays all of the strengths, habits, and flaws of my generation.

Not very long ago I was in the first-class cabin on an airplane. Here was the view from my seat:

All the Gen-Zers, twelve to sixteen years old, were watching things on their cell phones while wearing headphones. None of them used tablets.

All the Millennials and Gen-Xers used tablets and laptops.

Baby Boomers were on laptops (if they weren't sleeping).

The Gen-Zers ordered water to drink, or some kind of juice. Most of them turned down the warm nuts and the lunch meal of roasted veggies and quinoa or salmon salad, yuck! There were no other options. Instead, they brought their own snacks they had stored in their backpacks, mostly chips. These kids even turned down the warm chocolate-chip cookies that were offered.

All the Gen-Zers, girls and boys, wore comfortable sneakers, sweatpants, and pullover hoodies. The girls were clearly wearing hoodies from the "boy" section of the store—not one had one in pink or any other so-called "girl" color.

Every Gen-Zer carried a backpack on board—no carry-on suitcases, bags, duffle bags, etc. For both girls and boys, it was backpacks all the way. And none of them used the overhead compartments to stow their backpacks. They kept them under their seats for easy accessibility.

In addition to the snacks, all the Gen-Zers' backpacks were fully equipped with cords, chargers, backup chargers, and headphones (mostly the fat, comfy ones, like Beats, with an earbud pair for backup). None of them used the earphones the airline provided wrapped in those tiny clear packages. No need to provide them anymore!

This was a three-hour flight from Philadelphia to Miami, and none of the Gen-Zers slept. They were all entertained instead, watching content on their phones. The flight had no Internet, so they had shows, movies, and games downloaded. Most of the parents slept!

This bunch of Gen-Zers were zero work for the airplane crew.

They required nothing from them. There was no communication necessary between Gen-Z passengers and the crew. They kept to themselves, and didn't ask any questions or complain about the air conditioner, the heat, the lights, etc. Nothing.

We were all completely self-sufficient. That's who our generation is. We bring everything we need. We amuse ourselves. We are not needy; we figure out how to work things before we ask someone for help.

Another thing I noticed was that none of the Gen-Zers talked to the neighbor sitting next to them. They never removed their headphones or made eye contact. They minded their own business and kept to themselves. All was quiet.

Just as we aren't needy passengers, we also aren't social passengers. You won't be hearing anyone's life story on an airplane ride from this generation. Unlike the Millennial group of women talking loudly amongst themselves, excited about their vacation!

Also unlike my Gen-X mother, who spoke to an Italian man (a stranger) pretty much the whole flight. After one hour they knew each other's life stories. She learned everything—from hearing about his journey to America from Rome twenty-five years ago to looking at pictures of his retirement house and the view from his room on St. Croix in the Virgin Islands. There wasn't a topic they didn't touch!

After the flight they even hugged like old friends.

(How do I know all of this info? My mother spent the entire Uber ride from the Miami airport to our hotel in South Beach telling me what they'd spoken about. I was pretty much trapped into hearing about it, lol.)

It's like one of us is an alien race. There are those generations who share verbally, telling their life stories and their family history, showing family pictures. They talk about their experiences, their work life and their family life, their heritage, their values… And then there's our generation, who visually shares with one another through pics and videos—and not even necessarily our own personal pics and videos. In fact, we often share videos we watch and pics of things we like, but we don't get personal.

We are polite if you ask us a question, but we will not offer any information voluntarily. We don't just come out and share that our parents are divorced and our mother lives with her new boyfriend and we moved in with our dad, or that our dog died, or that our brother is on drugs and our sister's husband left her for his secretary, etc.

We don't share our personal lives openly with strangers like that, or even necessarily with each other. We just mind our own business; we don't like to bring attention to ourselves. This is why we like interactions, especially transactions, to be seamless and convenient, which we'll talk a lot more about in the following chapters.

A New Way to Hang Out

MILLENNIALS WERE DIFFERENT FROM EVERY other generation in that they were all about texting and instant gratification, convenience and speed.

Well, I know people didn't think it was possible, but things have changed again with this next generation. We may be shy with strangers, but with each other, Gen-Zers prefer to talk in real time.

This is why we like FaceTime so much, which, btw, is like the Antichrist to older generations. For Gen-Xers like my mom, God forbid she isn't prepared for one of us to be FaceTiming and someone sees her not looking good. She will freak out on you.

Baby Boomers like my dad, on the other hand…might just take your phone away while you're video-ing him and throw it in the trash! Just sayin.

When my siblings are home from college, it constantly sounds like they have friends over. They are always talking to one friend or another, and they bring that friend wherever they go. Recently I heard my sister talking to a friend while curling their hair in the bathroom. That's a perfect example of how different our generation is: what my mother didn't know was that they weren't just talking on the phone; my sister had her phone propped up on a towel, wedged between a pack of baby wipes and a brush, and they were FaceTiming.

My mother proceeded to enter the bathroom to put towels away.

The next thing you heard coming from the bathroom was my mother hollering at my sister for not warning her that the friend was on FaceTime while my sister was curling her hair.

"What if I wasn't decent? And your friend is live right in here with you! I thought you were on the phone!"

"Mom, I'm on the phone! Say hi, Grace!"

Mommy was not happy. She feels like it is off-the-charts insane to have your friend right there on FaceTime waiting for you to finish curling your hair.

But this is how Gen-Zers have a lot of our friends over. We are fine with that way of communication and interaction.

My father will say, "Call them back later." Like it's just a conversation.

This isn't just a conversation we are having with our friends, though. This is us hanging out with our friends when we physically can't be with them! We are not having a quick conversation, like our parents think. No, our friend is *over at our house*, visiting in real time. We could be connected for hours while one of us cleans the room or does our hair or cooks an entire meal.

It's not just girls, and it's not just young Gen-Zers, like me. My older brother is the same way. He props his phone up on a sneaker box and socks to keep it from slipping off the table in his room. He'll be watching a soccer game and talking about going to a concert and looking up concert tickets on his laptop, all with his friend sitting right there on the phone. Gen-Zers stay on FaceTime even if they aren't talking the entire time. It's about the experience. Neither party is lonely while the friend is present on FaceTime. They actually feel connected and go about their business, doing the same things they would do if the friend was sitting in the room with them.

Even Xbox Live on headphones isn't enough—Gen-Zers want to see each other playing. They want the visual, the closeness. A Gen-Xer has to look pretty to do it, and a Baby Boomer won't get on video at all, but with Gen Z it's all the time.

Neither Millennials nor any other generation had this kind of virtually intrusive lifestyle. If a friend was over they were actually in your house. Or even if you were IMing, back in the day, you sat at your computer and chatted.

Today, Gen-Zers carry their friends wherever they go and can share the entire visual experience with them.

Alexa, Cortana, and Siri, Oh My!

Watch your back, Google!

Remember when I mentioned that speaking is back in the Gen Z world? Well, it's back in a big way. Now not only are we able to ask Siri questions, but most households are bringing home Alexa and Cortana as well. All of the above are voice activated, which means…no more Googling!

It sounds shocking, but we like to just ask the question out loud. "Hey Alexa, when was the Spanish-American War?" No more having to type for Gen-Zers!

Gen-Zers also already use the microphone in our cell phones to dictate texts, emails, notes, and anything else you can think of.

Of course, being dyslexic, I think these oral features are almost better than the invention of ice cream. I don't have to type anything. Ever!

I just dictate, and the software for this keeps getting better and better. Mistakes are fewer with each update, and it keeps getting more convenient.

We don't have to look up football scores for our fathers anymore: "Alexa, what was the score of the Eagles game?" And we can just have fun with her, too: "Alexa, how old is LeBron James?"

My prediction is that everything will be voice activated, at least within the home. You won't pull out your phone or sit down at your laptop; you will just speak commands and they will be granted.

What a wonderful world we live in! And it's only getting better, smarter, and more sophisticated. One day we will all have smart houses where everything will be run by the sound of our voice. It brings an entirely new dimension to the phrase "Use your voice," doesn't it? Our generation welcomes all of this technology with open arms.

Every Day is Present-Worthy for Gen Z

I'M NOT SAYING THAT HOLIDAYS or birthdays are going to become nonexistent, but with Generation Z, those days of waiting for that special Christmas or birthday present are long gone.

We are the instant-gratification generation. I have read many articles that say retailers are waiting until Generation Z reaches their peak spending years. You retailers have it all wrong!

I need you to know there are no such years. Those years are now, today. If your child is old enough to go to school, then they are seeing what the other kids have and *will* find a way to get you to purchase those items. We are gifted today.

Here's an example: my friend just received an Oculus VR headset for no reason, just because he has the gift of persistence. And I just received a 3D printer because I texted my father a persuasive essay a few days a week for two weeks.

So do not wait until we have our own money to start marketing to us—we are much more willing to spend our parents' money than our own! You must learn how we operate now. We are professionals at convincing our parents to make purchases outside of holidays. I'm just thirteen and I know every available new gadget, device, sneaker, you name it, out there. Our parents aren't up on things like we are.

Since I got the 3D printer, I've been printing objects for six days straight and have made a minimum of $45 per day selling them at school. When my father found out I was earning money, he said, "Are you going to start paying me back for the 3D printer?"

I said, "That wasn't in the deal when you purchased it."

While we love to earn our own money and will find multiple ways to do so, we aren't quick to part with our own money like we will our parents' money. It's not that we're cheap, but that we like to save our money and spend yours instead. It's pretty smart of us!

So, as you can clearly see, our peak spending years are not going to be when we start earning our own paycheck—we already get our parents to spend plenty of money on us on a daily basis. Call us the persuasive-texting generation. We will find a way to get what we want, even if we have to save all our allowances, wash cars, or sell our stuff on eBay, Shapeways, or Etsy.

We will find plenty of ways to get money for what we want before we start earning a paycheck, and no more waiting for our birthdays for this generation.

The Internet is open 24/7, and so is Generation Z's spending.

The Two-Fold Mess-Up

"Do what you do so well that they will want to see it again and bring their friends."

— Walt Disney

ONE OF THE BIGGEST THINGS you have to keep in mind with this generation is that when you mess up with us, it's two-fold.

Two-fold can mean "in two different ways," and it can also mean "twice the amount." A two-fold increase is a 100% increase. However...a two-fold decrease is also a 100% decrease.

Here's why it matters so much when you're dealing with Generation Z: we share everything in the form of a post. If we like your product or your customer service, we share a good post, and then whoever sees it is a potential new customer for you.

But if you screw up, the opposite is true. We will post negatively about your product and our bad experience with your customer service. Then you not only don't get the *good* post from us, but you also get all the negative retweets/reposts.

You will be in the post either way; it's up to you if it's a positive or negative post. In today's world, that can be way more than a 100% decrease. It's like two-fold in dog years.

The Customer is Never Right

HERE IS A PROBLEM IN today's business world that applies to all generations but will especially come back to bite you with your Gen Z customers:

When did it become "the customer is always wrong"?

When my parents owned businesses, customer service (CS) was their number-one priority. If they didn't have happy, content customers, they had no business. Which meant they had no money! It's as easy as that.

But today, customer service is a huge problem. Companies and businesses are suffering more than they actually realize because of poor CS, in both their brick-and-mortar stores and their online support.

My parents' families ran their businesses by the saying "The customer is always right."

What happened to that saying in today's market? That line should stand forever!

I wonder who is training CS departments today, because when you ask for a manager they get even fresher than their employees. They don't seem to care that "this call is being recorded for quality assurance." Apparently no one ever really goes back and listens to the recordings, because if they did their employees would be much better behaved. And how about emailing a company's support team? They actually want to argue back with you through email.

Here is the problem: no one takes ownership today; no one knows how to say, "I'm sorry." When you call or email to complain about a product, no one starts off with or even ends with an apology. They don't give you a coupon or a percentage off your next purchase.

Furthermore, they don't care if you are inconvenienced by either their faulty product or problems with their support. Let's say you take off work and wait on house arrest from ten to three for them to come fix something. If you call and complain that they are past their given five-hour window, they will just say, "Oh, well, if you can't wait, we will just reschedule!"

Are you kidding me? Instead of owning up to their problem, they have an attitude.

For example, recently an appliance company was scheduled to fix our washer and they never showed up. When my mother called to find out what had happened, the CS rep said, "Oh, we had you scheduled for a different date."

My mother was appalled. Not only had she had taken off a day of work for nothing, but we also *still* needed our washer fixed. Yet all the CS rep could say was that the scheduler must have "messed up." She didn't apologize, and she didn't even offer to waive the house-call fee or discount our next bill.

When my mother expressed that their lack of empathy for this rather huge mistake was shocking, the CS rep said, "Do you want me to send someone out or not, and then you can find someone else to fix your washer?"

Like a threat!

My mother said it was unfathomable that she was spoken to this way—and this was a huge commercial company. There should be accountability. The first words out of their mouth should have been something along the lines of, "I'm so sorry that you encountered this." Yet they acted as if they just don't want our business.

Do they really not need us? No; that's not how a business works.

You must train your staff and CS department to apologize first, because "the customer is always right," and to then address the problem or issue.

It seems that companies are spending less and less on CS departments and outsourcing their support to other countries to save money, but this is a complete disaster. My parents knew every facet of their family businesses and how they ran, because their fathers showed them and let them have responsibility. They knew the customers and treated them like gold, because that was the only reason they had successful businesses in the first place: they had happy customers. They made sure the customer always came first. This is not a part of the company that you should be outsourcing to complete strangers in foreign countries, who hardly know your business and simply reply "My bad" when they screw up on a support call.

Instead, you should be spending more on better support, as consumer retention is becoming more and more difficult. It's not time to cut back in this area. You should be kissing up to us like never before, and to do that you need to bring back the empathy and caring behind your products. Train high-quality CS people to represent your companies, and make sure these representatives know how to talk, text, and empathize with people.

Furthermore, as your newest generation of customers, we don't even want to be wasting our time composing an email, chatting, or calling support. Our time is very important to us, so we want to simply text support, like www.livesupport.com; we can even send you pictures of the problem this way. Gen-Zers don't want to interact with you any more than we possibly have to. Any other type of support should be a thing of the past!

Customer service is an art. You have to stop treating the most important part of your business as the last thing you want to spend money on, or you will find yourselves with no company.

Unlike previous generations, Gen-Zers actually won't put up with this unacceptable behavior.

For example, we will not put up with being told by a CS rep something like "Your tablet is dead because you need to charge it!" Your customers are not idiots and don't want to be spoken to like this.

You know that you are only as good as your weakest link, so if you run a company, CS needs to be one of the strongest links. You need to keep on top of this; you should have your best people taking care of your precious customers.

If we aren't treated nicely we won't come back, and this is easily done because you are not the only game in town.

It should be your priority, because the Internet makes it easy to review and leave feedback—and Gen-Zers love to give it!

Hidden Fees at Checkout

DON'T TRY TO BE SNEAKY with us—don't wait till we get to our cart to charge us with hidden fees. For example, we don't want to spend the time customizing something and then find as we're checking out that the price has suddenly jumped from $17.50 to $26.50. We love to personalize things, and adding our name to something shouldn't be punished by a hidden charge. Instead, update the price on the add-to-cart page! You will only get us angry when we go to check out and see this new, surprise price.

Guess what? That's why we abandon carts! Most of the time it's because something got us angry.

Similarly, don't tell us one shipping and delivery date when we're adding something to our cart and then surprise us with a completely different date at checkout. Or, better yet, some stores send a completely different delivery date in the confirmation email, so we don't catch it at all and find ourselves waiting for a delivery that isn't coming. Btw—Gen-Zers don't do email!

Sometimes we are even hit with a post-Christmas delivery date when we're clearly shopping for Christmas presents. Why would you want to do that to a customer? It is so unethical to trick us into an order with a false promise. You know we want the product by Christmas, you show us a delivery date of December 23, and then you change the date to December 29 when we're reviewing our order in checkout. Sometimes we even miss the updated delivery date and hit order anyway, but who would want the item after Christmas?

This is a deceitful tactic, and a waste of our time. What's more, in most cases, had we known ahead of time the true delivery date, we would actually have paid more for an earlier delivery if that were an option. But now, knowing you are willing to scam us after we've already put our credit card info in, we are completely turned off not just by your online store but also by your company in general, and we will run from you, not walk.

Almost nothing will turn us off more than deceit. You have to understand that our time is more precious to us than ever before. So while previous generations may have fallen for this sort of deceit, we will not. We notice everything, and once you've made this sort of bad impression on us, we will not only abandon the cart—and your store—but also spread the word. Back in the day this meant rumors—today this means slamming you on social media. And don't forget, our friends listen.

These surprise delivery dates and hidden charges are examples of the two-fold mess-up. You failed the sale and you turned away tons of potential customers, and opened yourself up to being smeared across all social media platforms. Keep in mind, sharing can be a wonderful thing—or not!

"Luxury" Hanging on by a Thread

REMEMBER WHEN I SAID WHAT a turnoff hidden fees at checkout are? The same goes for these stores that charge $2,000 for a luxury item and then want to charge you $20 to ship it. Recently my dad's friend was on a trip to Las Vegas with his friends and bought his wife a beautiful handbag. When he asked them to ship it home, they wanted to add an extra charge.

That is such a turnoff. Just suck it up and pay it yourself, or at least put it in the total purchase price ahead of time.

My dad's friend almost didn't buy the bag because they wanted to charge a lousy $20 for shipping! That's not how you treat customers, especially high-end customers who are already paying a fortune for your products. They don't want to feel like they are responsible for a boring detail like shipping, and they don't want to feel deceived by being slapped with a hidden charge at the end. Now my father's buddy is going to write a scathing review about paying stupid shipping charges for a multi-thousand-dollar luxury item.

It's all relative. If we've spent thousands of dollars, twenty bucks should be nothing to you. Just eat it! That is called courtesy to the customer. You are a high-end luxury brand—act like it.

You know that when we walk into your store to order something we don't want to have to carry bags around with us. We like to have our purchases delivered, so when we get home from vacation, or even just home from shopping, the box is there waiting for us.

Make sure your brand is making a difference in every step of the purchase process. Make it a seamless, pleasant transaction.

Be Accountable for Your Inventory

WE WANT YOU TO HAVE everything you say you do.

Keep your site updated; keep your store updated. We take the information on websites at face value, assuming it to be true, up to date, and honest. If we get to your store and feel you lied to us about your stock, we are going to blow you up on social media, and NOT in a good way!

Simply be honest with us. Have what you say you have and update your site the second you run out of something—especially if you have a brick-and-mortar store! Gen-Zers never want to make a physical trip only to find out it was for nothing. Remember, we are checking the status of your product on our phones every second up until we walk into your store, so to find out it isn't there a second later feels doubly deceitful.

Another tip: make your website mirror your physical store/dealership. Let us have a video tour so we can see everything we want to visit. We like to see places and know what it's like before we get there. That way we'll walk into a dealership and know how to navigate it like we work there! We will know where you keep every car if you are true to your website.

We don't want to wander around aimlessly looking for something in your store only to find out you sold it or don't have any in stock. Don't make us show up in hopes that we will just buy something else. We want what we want, and will feel like you made us come there under false pretenses if we find out you don't actually have it.

Website Welcomes

I CONSULT FOR NUMEROUS BUSINESSES. One service I'm often hired to provide is looking over a business's website. I tell them what I like, what they need or are missing, what I don't like, what I would add, why I would go back, if it's easy to navigate, if it holds my attention, if I understand what the business is about…

Honestly, Gen-Zers are not big with websites in general.

So when Gen-Zers are Googling something specific and your company comes up in a search, if we click on your site and have zero idea what you are selling or what your site is about within the first six-second scan, we are gone!

Other times we are really determined to find a product that interests us, so we search around your site for this product you say you have, only to find out that you are a commercial distributor and do not sell to the general public. That makes us very angry, as you totally wasted our time by not stating on your first page that you are a "commercial distributor" and regular people cannot buy from you!

Tell us that right off the bat.

Your website should not be a guessing game for visitors.

Don't Hide Your Buttons

Some websites have no social media widgets. Or sometimes the widgets are kept in a drop-down, like in the About Us category.

How would anyone know they are there? I can assure you Gen-Zers are not going to waste time looking around for them.

Why would web designers hide the social media buttons? You need to have them in plain sight, especially on your mobile site.

If I'm on a car-dealer website, for example, I want to be able to click on a visible YouTube video. We need to see a play button, or you need to at least lead us to one in hopes that we will watch the video, comment on it, and share it.

This is yet another example of how businesses need to get the right web designer who is skilled in *all* aspects of design, social media, and marketing, not just someone who knows how to build a basic site.

I Am Not a Robot

ONE PROBLEM I SEE THAT is insane is that many sites still use CAPTCHAs, where you have to prove you're not a robot by reading the distorted numbers and letters and retyping them.

Are you kidding me?

First of all, the numbers and letters are different sizes and often overlapping each other—that is hard enough. Second, I was just on a major game site today, and I won't mention any names but this site actually showed you the crazy number/letter code and then took you to *another screen* to enter it.

Who the heck approved that one?

Do you really expect us to remember that code and then type it in on a different screen?

My brother used five curse words trying to get into this site. Thankfully, I thought of just taking a pic of the code with my phone so he could go to the next page to enter it!

The takeaway: Wow, that was an insane amount of effort. If it weren't a huge gaming site we wouldn't go back in a million years.

Ad-Blocker Kings

GENERATION Z WILL BE THE kings of ad-blocking.

First of all, we rarely visit websites, and when we do we aren't going to put up with ads jumping all over the page to distract us.

We don't like ads on YouTube, either; in fact, we will more than likely pay for adblocking services, as we would rather pay up front to not have to see them and be distracted by them.

Advertisers of the future will be paid for people *not* watching their ads. Who would have ever guessed that was a possibility?

We do not want to see pop-ups. Do not have things jumping out at us or sliding from side to side. Do not ever have an ad move around the page and block us from what we are reading. We are not the type to hit the tiny X in the corner of that box to remove the ad. Instead we'll click the big X and get off your site completely and it will remain imprinted on our brain to never visit your site again.

You get no second chances with us.

If you want advertisers floating all over your page, you will lose us completely. Everything distracts us. It's not that we *can't* navigate through them but that we *don't want* to hold our curser to the side so your ads don't stalk and cover the content we are trying to read.

I see top sites doing this—I'm talking business entrepreneurial websites—and they are unbearable to look at. The site becomes so cluttered it looks like it's just for ads.

We also do not want to chat with your website CS, so don't harass us while we are looking for something. If you piss us off right off the bat with that "How can we help you?" chat window as soon as we click on your site, that's how fast we are clicking off. It's like the lady at a department store stalking you, asking if she can help you. We will call you over if we need help. Get away from us!

We *would* like to be able to text you our questions, but we do not want to have to chat, email, or call.

And another thing: we will never provide our email to enter your site! Nothing more to say on that topic.

STOP Texting Campaigns!

GEN-ZERS AREN'T SERIAL TEXTERS (WE prefer FaceTime), but that doesn't mean we mind texting with our friends. It does mean that we like to choose who we want to receive texts from.

Which means that campaigns through texting is something most of us can't stand.

We don't mind a simple text from our doctor's office reminding us of our upcoming appointment tomorrow, or from our baseball team reminding us of the game time and location. That's something we invited. But we dislike with a passion when stores text us notifications, even if they are for a sale. We find that so annoying. We don't wish to receive a text from stores we shopped from.

Only our friends or contacts text us. We find anyone else texting us an intrusion of our privacy. We don't want to see a random text from a number we don't know. Even if your store is inviting us to a holiday sale, it doesn't feel like a reminder about an opportunity—it feels like a stranger showing up on our phones.

STOP!

That is what we text you back. Most text campaigns say, "Text STOP if you would like to stop receiving texts from this sender."

Well, we immediately text, STOP.

We want to stop the madness. We didn't give you permission to text us, you are not our friend, and we even feel like you must have stolen our number somehow, because we definitely did not give you permission to use it with the intent to text-stalk us.

Not the way to win Gen-Zers over.

Who Dumped My Shopping Cart?

STOP DUMPING OUR SHOPPING CARTS!

Do you know why Amazon is king? I'll say it again and again: not because they have the best prices, but because they will leave stuff in your cart indefinitely. Even if they change the prices of the items, even if you don't go back for months.

You wonder why some huge department stores are going bye-bye? They dump your cart if you leave the page or even just stop being active on it for a few minutes.

Are you kidding me? Are you trying to go out of business?

For example, while Christmas shopping at a certain store online one evening, my mother went to my closet to check my shirt size. When she got back on her iPad, her cart was empty. She freaked out. I swear she was crying. She said she'd been shopping for an hour, she'd picked out thirteen different items for different people, that was her last item, and there was no way she was doing it all over again. It has happened to me as well: I put things in my cart and by the time I can get my mother to see the stuff, it's gone—empty cart!

Why are you so eager to empty our carts? Don't you know things come up while we are shopping? Maybe our boss walks in, or we have baseball practice, or we have to take a shower. That doesn't give you the right to punish us and dump our cart; you have nothing to gain from that. I will never go to another site that doesn't hold things in my cart for at least a few days.

I Spy

"Zoom functionality brought an entire new meaning to stalking."
— Sky Rota

LET ME TELL YOU WHAT a perfect world looks like through a Gen-Zer's eyes.

We look at a posted picture, and everything in that picture is clickable and for sale!

It's that simple. You have the answer!

But I will continue.

We find it really frustrating when we can kind of see something we want in a picture, but it's not labeled and we can't zoom in to find out more information about it. We want the ability to click on anything within that pic and be taken to a checkout cart to buy it, or at least to a store to have the option to purchase it once we see how much it costs.

We need to be able to buy anything we see. Anything on your website. Everything in the background of your posted photos.

You have no idea how many people zoom in on my posted pics or videos and ask me what sneakers I am wearing, what car or toy is on my desk. And I always tell my visitors and subscribers the answers to the questions they ask.

You have to remember we are visual today. Instagram started letting you zoom in on pics because they know we want to zoom in on everything! We want to see what's in the background. We want everything we see to be accessible to us. So you must make everything in the pic clickable and purchasable.

If you don't believe me, try testing it out: put something in the background that may pique someone's interest and watch how many people contact you about it.

It doesn't even have to be the object itself—try placing a tiny sign in the background saying, "free diamond earrings with a $200 purchase." Try to almost hide it, as if you don't want people to see it, and then sit back and see how many people zoom in on the pic, find it, and ask you about it. Seriously!

Paperless World

GENERATION Z HAS GROWN UP in a virtually paperless world. To us paper is just something to recycle. Snail mail and checks are a thing of the past.

More and more of our schools and workplaces are going completely paperless. We email our teachers/professors/bosses/coworkers, and sometimes text them. Our grades are posted online, and we (or our parents) receive text alerts from our doctors, orthodontists, Little League coaches, and veterinarians.

If it were up to us we would remove all mailboxes, as they are just small trash-collector boxes to us. We never think to check it when my Baby Boomer dad is out of town. The only thing we like to see being delivered through the mail is a package. (And don't you think it's time to make them look more appealing? We're receiving more packages than ever, and yet the plain old brown cardboard box is still the standard after all these years. Can someone add some color? Anyone?)

One of the things this means is that we do not ever need to go to a bank. We look at our bank balances online. We transfer money from one account to another or pay bills online. We use PayPal and similar services to lend money, share a payment, or pay back a friend. We buy textbooks and tickets to concerts online. We receive our paychecks from our bosses or allowance money from our parents through direct deposit. Our grandparents give us gift cards on the holidays. We never carry cash or checks.

First of all, Gen-Zers don't even learn cursive, so we wouldn't even be able to sign our name on a check. We have zero clue what a check looks like or how to fill one out. When we open a bank account, we never order checks.

Because it's a paperless world, most of our parents don't carry cash anymore, and one thing this means is that younger Gen-Zers have no way of carrying money on them. So banks need to get with the times and lower the age limit for getting a debit card! They can still have monetary limits on them.

It's 2017, I'm thirteen, and I need my own debit card with my own name on it.

How else am I supposed to go into a store and pay for something without my parents being there? When I want to buy something, I have no cash on me, and my mom is sitting in the car; she doesn't want to come in the store, and she doesn't have cash on her either.

Our parents have no cash to hand us when we go to a movie with a friend. And only certain places, like laser tag, let you pay over the phone beforehand. This is inconvenient not just for us but also for our parents.

Banks are looking for a way to start attracting us—it's time for them to start thinking about how they expect the kids under driver's-license age to carry money. Someone's going to need to figure out a form of ID for us to show who we are. There's lots of work to do.

Realistic Real Estate

WHAT IS WITH THE TWENTY-FIVE-PICTURE maximum on top real-estate websites? And why can't they incorporate the zoom feature?

We want to see pictures of every single room in that house, apartment, or commercial space, and we want to be able to zoom in and inspect every detail of the property.

If they say two-car parking, we need to see the garage. If there is an elevator, we want to see the inside of it. If there are four closets, we need to see each one. We don't want to read the list of amenities; we want to see all of them.

In addition, every listing should include videos of the property as well as of the living/commercial space. We don't want to have to find the property on Google Earth—save us the time by presenting every inch of it in a video. If there's a great yard or a special park across the street, we want to see it. We want to know what it looks like when you're walking through the front door.

There should be no guesswork. We should be able to see all aspects of the property visually.

And what this means for all you property owners is that you are going to have to invest more in fixing up your properties. Increase their salability/rentability. For homeowners, I suspect that house staging is going to rise significantly.

For apartment owners, if you're not the greatest landlord, you should remember that we have already Googled reviews of your building. We've already found out how well you maintain your properties, how you treat your tenants, how accessible you are, etc.

On that note, do you landlords even check the reviews of your properties? The answer often seems to be no—I can't tell you how many times I've seen the same complaints posted in new reviews year after year: "smelly," "dark scary hallways with zero lighting," "washer and dryer never work," "trash room stinks throughout the entire hallway."

Well, Gen-Zers are the review kings, so letting those reviews slide will no longer work. We won't be renting disgusting apartments that are completely neglected. Nothing gets past us—we will see that people have been leaving poor reviews for the past six years, and we will never even consider your building *or* your management company.

So it's time to start upping your game. You've had plenty of time to make those negative reviews positive ones; don't say I didn't warn you.

TripAdvisor: To Comment or Not to Comment

Reviews can be your enemy—or not.

TripAdvisor is the largest social media platform for hotels, restaurants, and attractions.

Do any of your hotels and restaurants get this? Your most important social platform is not just a pic posted on Instagram with #prettygarden. It is, by far, TripAdvisor!

Yet it doesn't seem like this is being taught in hotel- and restaurant-management school. Well, hopefully they are teaching Gen-Zers these courses today. There is no more powerful a tool than receiving live feedback.

My own mother is a top TripAdvisor reviewer. I have no idea what badges she has, but I can tell you she is very proud of her writing skills and has over a million people reading her reviews.

But why is it not every company's practice to reply to every review? Do you know how impolite it is to receive comments and not reply? How can you be so rude as to ignore your guests?

Communicating with your clients/customers should be your number-one priority, as it is part of the art of customer service. You should feel lucky that they are giving you free information (answers) regarding how to make your business better, or complimenting what you are already doing well. This is the greatest tool you can have for your business: immediate feedback without asking (begging) your guests to fill out a questionnaire. You are getting feedback straight from their experience. They took the time to write the review; your company needs to appreciate this opportunity for receiving voluntary feedback! You should have your concierge writing replies every single day as part of their job description.

You need to understand that this is all part of social media. I don't know why so many companies don't realize that.

TripAdvisor can honestly make or break your business. More than three hundred million travelers use TripAdvisor each month. My family has avoided certain excursions and hotels specifically due to TripAdvisor reviews.

High-End Hotel Internet:

HIGH-END MEANS SUPERIOR, TOP OF the line, first-rate.

So why, when we check into a high-end hotel, are you being cheap about your Wi-Fi? It is wrong to charge your guests for daily wireless Internet on top of what they're paying.

Just put it in the price of the room. No one wants to see a charge for Internet as if it's a "luxury" amenity. It is no longer a luxury; it's a necessity.

What's almost worse is offering the slow Internet for free and the "super-speedy" Internet for $19.99 a day! No one wants slow Internet, so it is ridiculous and insulting to even offer it, much less to pretend like you're doing us a favor by including it for free.

Stop Blocking Kid Lux Lifestyle

TODAY, PARENTS HAVE THEIR KIDS with them constantly. They take them everywhere, including to get manicures and pedicures with them, boys and girls alike.

Yet five-star luxury hotels will turn these kids away from their fantastic spas. That's a missed opportunity.

I'm not talking about offering full-body massages to young kids. I'm talking about how I can get my foot massaged during a pedicure with my mom, but I can't enter a hotel's luxury spa to get a foot massage with my parents. Is there a law against this, or is this just the old-fashioned approach?

You have to start early to hook this generation. How are you going to expect us to learn and enjoy a luxury lifestyle if you don't allow us to experience it until after age sixteen? Do you seriously need to be old enough to have a driver's license just to get a foot massage at a luxury spa? Foot massages and back massages are available at any other lower-end place, but not at a luxury hotel spa.

Why?

You have to realize that we are all about experiences today. We want to try these things. If we can afford them, why are you turning away money?

Someone needs to check into this and start making luxury hotel spas kid-friendly, at least for ages twelve and up. Add treatments for us to your spa menu. Welcome us into that luxury world.

This isn't just for us. You will also gain more adult customers, as sometimes parents don't want to leave their kids unattended at a resort or hotel, even when they are twelve and up...sometimes especially when they are twelve and up. If you can't accommodate the kid, then the parents can't go.

Of course, I understand that parents often go to the spa to get away from their kids and relax. I'm not saying you have to have parents and kids side by side. Separate them, and offer kid-friendly treatments like foot and hand massages. And how about introducing us to a facial treatment—how hard is it to wash our face?

It's a win-win. You keep your adult customers and even gain more. You seriously need to re-think the demographics of the luxury lifestyle. Welcome us, and we will share you like crazy!

Selling an Experience

ABOVE ALL, GEN-ZERS WANT THE experience over anything else. So take the opportunity to wow us. Let us have fun.

While wealthy people can buy whatever they want, living an experience can be more satisfying—it lets them let go and have a good time and not have to be uptight. It's likely that they typically are uptight and busy all the time, so give them some fun, and make it real! They want to see how the other half—"regular people"—have fun.

That's why Richard Branson always looks happy—because he is having fun.

Shut off the lights and let them play laser tag and give whoever wins a present. Rich people love to get free stuff! Let them win a Rolex or a driver for a dinner out in a Rolls-Royce.

Give them a memorable night over anything.

Let the women take their shoes off and unwind and make them feel special—give them foo-foo slippers to make them feel like a princess.

Or serve warm chocolate-chip cookies to make them feel like a kid. Pipe the smell of brownies or cotton candy into the room. Let them smell good memories.

Be their friend. The ease of text marketing combined with special connection is what they want. Attention is what they are seeking.

On top of providing the experience, you should also focus on letting us take it home with us. Everything should be for sale today.

Hotels, for example, could be earning far more money with this move.

If we stay at a place we like, we don't want to just go into the hotel gift shop and purchase a shirt with your logo. We probably aren't shopping in that physical store anyway, but we will check out your online store, so you need to have one. You should be selling memories!

Hotels can sell everything their guests encounter during their stay. The soaps and shampoo, towels and robes, sheets and pillows, bedding, even the mattress. Furniture, bathroom mirrors, blow dryers, shower caps—you name it and your guests will want to buy it. Not something similar to it, but the real deal that we had in the room during our vacation. We want to be able to purchase the experience we felt on our visit.

Smells Make Memories

ONCE WE TOOK A VACATION to sunny Miami, Florida. We were so excited on the plane there. Finally the captain got on the intercom and said we would be landing in Miami in twenty minutes, and the moment he did, my mother applied this tropical hand lotion.

The scent of fresh coconut float through the plane just enough to make everyone smile. They could feel the smell of vacation coming.

Wow, what a nice surprise. Any island-themed trip could use this tropical-scented blast.

Businesses, stores, apartment buildings, hotels, office building common areas, gyms—any commercial area where customers gather—should all be thinking of using companies like ScentAir, which uses olfactory (sense of smell) marketing to improve a customer's experience in a place.

People develop strong feelings and memories about a place based on its smell, so why not make the smell memory a good one?

You really don't want your airplane smelling like raw onions from your neighbor's hoagie, or BO from someone across the aisle. My father always remembers how some casinos smell disgusting from the smoke and sweat and odors from people who've been sitting there all night.

When you walk into a plane, casino, or any business, you want to smell something pleasant and welcoming and even familiar.

Believe me; I am a nose person, and come from a long line of people with sensitive noses.

We remember the smell of our grandmother baking, and we also remember the mildew smell from a restaurant that used a sour-smelling rag to wipe the table down with. We won't be going back there, but we will be going back to the hotel with the lobby that always smelled like simple fresh flowers.

Business can get almost any scent, from leather to cookies to clean fresh sheets. You could use the scent of baby powder to sell baby products. Or a custom-made scent for any kind of luxury product.

You must get with the times and try to influence all of our senses.

I hope to see/smell more of this in the future.

#MarketingDisasters

ONE OF THE MOST COMMON wastes of a marketing budget is not knowing your demographics.

#doyourresearch

For example: just because a hotel is high-end doesn't mean it's the right place for you to launch, promote, or even advertise your new "high-end" product.

Not long ago, while on vacation at a family-friendly luxury hotel, I ended up being present at the launch of a high-end champagne. They had half-naked girls dancing around the pool…but the problem was, at the same time there were thirty kids thirteen and under playing and swimming with their water wings on.

It was a total disaster. The husbands were trying to take videos of the girls and their wives were covering their husbands' eyes. The moms were dragging their kids out of the pool literally with the pink-flamingo floaties still stuck around their waists!

This was a two-fold fail. Their shtick was to give people a collectible champagne flute embossed with their logo and have them post to social media with a special hashtag. Well, no one was posting anything except for all the moms, who were saying how inappropriate this launch was! They took their kids out of the pool, brought their lunches to their hotel rooms, and blasted the champagne brand on social media. And I'm positive those guests also ended up writing scathing letters to the hotel management about how inappropriate this event was for families with children staying at a family resort.

This was a disastrous marketing plan and total waste of money. No one looked at the demographics of the actual clientele of this hotel: this was a luxury family hotel, not a clubbing site—no singles!

This is an example of why you need to make sure you research your demographics long before you just assume a high-end product should be launched at a high-end facility/venue. #totalwasteofmarketing$

There are many other factors you must consider:

You must have the proper people planning an event like this, first of all; you need much more than just an "event planner" to "promote" your new product.

You have to research what other products have been promoted or launched at a venue before you book it. Check a venue's social media first to see if they've had successful launches for products that are similar to yours or that target the same demographic. For example, if this company had glanced at the hotel's Instagram posts, as I did the second the launch went bad, they would have seen that it posted photos of weddings, food, babies, families, palm trees, and kids playing in the swimming pool.

Whoever thought of this disaster should be fired for not doing their homework and wasting a launch, not to mention all that money.

There was not a single indication that this hotel would have the champagne brand's target demographic, partying singles, as its clientele. I was twelve and it took me less than one minute to do the research and conclude that this was the wrong venue for that type of event.

It's time to seriously rethink your marketing teams. They need to be able to do this research.

Tasteful Advertising

ADVERTISING CAMPAIGNS TODAY CAN BE funny, edgy, and progressive, but whatever you do, don't make them trashy.

I constantly notice that some of your ads are just sooo irrelevant to the product.

We don't need to see two girls kissing one guy or girls on top of each other in an ad that is so focused on PDA we can't even tell what it's trying to sell. Why do you think it helps to portray people in that trashy, negative manner?

I especially see these sorts of ads for high-end luxury products, and I most commonly see something like two half-dressed girls hanging all over each other and groping each other. One, for example, was an ad for earrings, with each girl displaying a different pair.

But there was no need to show these girls like that. First of all, it has nothing to do with the jewelry. Second of all, it shows the jewelry in a tasteless way, and I don't think it shows the girls in their personal best light. Thirdly, I respect men and women and same-sex couples, and I don't think these ads are being respectful to the LGBT community—or anyone for that matter.

We don't want to see couples being intimate in an ad for any product. All it does is turn us off of the product—we can't get past the picture. You have to keep in mind that this generation is made up of very visual-oriented consumers—but that just means we're more affected than ever by demeaning visuals in an ad.

We are used to seeing all kinds of couples—why do you think you need to exploit a same-gender couple to make your product look more "edgy"? All it does is make it classless. Any couple can look like they're having fun in an ad without having to engage in filthy PDA. We respect a tasteful layout a lot more. Let them look elegant when they are representing your product and company, and let us have a nice memory of the pic, not an inappropriate one. Take a classy pic of models wearing your products—or, better yet, how about real, everyday people? You can even ask your customers to send in pics of them showing off your products!

You have to understand that Gen-Zers have learned from the previous generation's mistakes. We learned from Millennials posting inappropriate pictures on social media that it was a complete disaster. So why do you print advertisers still show content that would get you fired from a job if it was posted on your personal social media account?

That is sooo ten years ago.

Please, keep your ads tasteful. No one wants to see anyone behaving poorly, let alone while representing a luxury brand to the public.

What Gen-Zers have learned: when in doubt, ask your grandma what she thinks of the picture.

Let Toys Be Toys

Stop the gender-specific marketing.

In your brick-and-mortar store, when you have blue aisles for "boy" toys and pink aisles for "girl" toys, this just tells your customers that you have to be that gender to go up that aisle. If you aren't, you feel awkward.

When you shop online, the same holds true. The categories are still "boy" and "girl."

You need to start embracing all kids, all people. Stop breaking us down into genders and telling us what we should be playing with, purchasing, or wearing. Why can't you just say toys are for "kids"? Why do toys have to have a gender?

I grew up with an older brother and two older sisters.

I played with all their toys. My first car I played with (and you know what an exotic car enthusiast I am today) was a Barbie car because that's all we had around our playroom. My brother was a dinosaur kid, I'm a car kid. So my only choice was the big Barbie car that my sisters had. It was great; I always liked how the doors could open so I could put my people in the car.

I also always wanted a toy house. Especially one of the ones that were decorated like it was Christmas time, with the doorbells that rang and the lights that lit up and other extras.

Most people would call this a "dollhouse." Including my parents.

But I didn't want to put "dolls" in it. I wanted a house to put my toy characters in, a garage to park my cars in. It didn't matter if Spider-Man and the Hulk, or aliens and SpongeBob, or the entire Avengers team lived in there. I didn't even mind the family that came with it. They were nice too.

The point is, girls aren't the only ones who want toy houses. And none of us need those super-pink or very girly-looking houses! Who in the world lives in a pink house? Where is that reality? (I'm an expert on realty sites, and I have never seen a pink house like that listed—just saying.)

I'm not saying you need to make "boy" houses. Just make a normal-looking house and make it available to everyone. In real life, men and women buy houses.

Plenty of girls want to play with Ninja Turtles and other characters that are stuck in the boy section. They also want to wear boys' sweatpants and sneakers. And just as I wanted to play with a toy house, girls want a toolset.

Another good example is the Easy-Bake oven. There is not a kid on the planet who didn't want one. It makes cake!

But they always put them in the "girl" category and made them girly-looking. So boys' parents didn't buy them for their sons. We had to suffer because you companies made it gender-specific forever! Like boys don't bake...

After a zillion years they started making a blue and then a black Easy-Bake oven, but the accessories are all still pink.

And why are toy strollers all still pink in 2017? There are plenty of dads out there pushing strollers with their babies in them, and they are all regular-colored strollers, yet if a little boy wants to push a toy stroller, they're all fufu pink. How do you expect us to be good fathers one day if you don't let us practice when we are little?

My mother let us have "babies," and pots and pans, and grocery shopping carts—whatever we wanted to play with. My grandmother taught my mother that it was okay to let boys hold baby dolls. If not, how else would they learn to hold their own baby one day? We played house and learned how to cook.

Nothing was just for girls or boys. My grandmother bought my aunt He-Man action figures and other "boy" heroes, and no one said a word to her about it. She raised strong daughters and a wonderful son who went on to have two daughters of his own and be a fantastic father.

My grandmother was forward-thinking and didn't place genders on toys.

Many companies still need to adopt this practice of inclusiveness. Generation Z is not composed of just two stereotypical genders. Stop putting us in two categories. This is not a pink and blue world anymore!

#lettoysbetoys

Gaming is for Everyone

DID YOU KNOW THAT WHEN video games were first invented, they were marketed to both male and female audiences? They weren't originally intended to be just for boys. Video game companies focused instead on marketing to kids *and* adults. Then at some point, Nintendo decided to focus almost exclusively on marketing to boys, and that decided the direction gaming culture took for decades.

Back in the 1970s, my mother played video games just as much as her brother. My aunt conquered Pac-Man.

When did things change?

I'll tell you when. When companies took the gaming consoles out of the electronic departments and put them in the "boy" aisle.

Why would companies start eliminating half our population from the market when that half loves playing games? Most people probably aren't aware that recent studies show that adult women are the largest demographic in the gaming industry. And they don't play "girl" games. They just want to be allowed to enjoy whatever games they enjoy without comments about our gender. Yet game companies go out of their way to make games "for boys" and to market only to male gamers.

Games are for everyone.

Judge a Brand by its Packaging

Remember that we are a visual generation—which means everything must look good!

Your packaging must look fantastic, from the box to the tissue paper inside. And yes, there does need to be a box.

Here's a typical example of a luxury brand messing up in that regard.

My mother recently bought handbags, wallets, and shoes from top designers (I won't mention any names) for my sisters, herself, and others for Christmas.

Out of the five high-end luxury brands she ordered from, only one sent their product in a box. None of the other products had any kind of designed packaging, let alone a cool, nice, or fancy box that you could store your product in or save for a collectible.

Instead, some of the items came in a cloth sack. Well, the sacks looked so cheap, with fuzzballs all over them, that we threw them out. These multi-thousand-dollar products came in cheap cloth sacks inside brown cardboard boxes.

That's it! Nothing special!

Are you kidding me with this horrible marketing? How do you forget about the packaging for these beautiful luxury products? I can't understand who dropped the ball at all these different luxury companies. Are you trying to save money?

My mother spent all that money and was actually sad when each package arrived! She was so let down that after she received two items from the same disappointing designer, she didn't even open the third cardboard box from them. Instead she wrote a scathing review about the company as well as emailed them to tell them what a disgrace they were.

The impression you give by having no packaging and throwing your expensive products in a crummy brown cardboard box is that they aren't worth anything and that their arrival is no big deal.

That is not an impression that keeps people coming back for more.

When you disappoint us, it's devastating to us. Because of the letdown, we often wish we hadn't bought the product. Had we known there was no packaging whatsoever, we probably wouldn't have.

You have to understand that this is not an area to skimp on. It's time to think of the consequences that are going to arise from your decision-making. I've mentioned that today, everything is seen through a lens, visually and publicly. It needs to look good so that we say good things about it. Had the packaging matched the level of design of the products, my mother would have taken pics of them to not only show her sister and friends but also post on social media. Those posts would have been shared (tons more exposure for the brand), and I would have done an "unveiling" YouTube video of her receiving and opening the box. Think how many more customers that could have gotten them!

But instead of sharing the news of the wonderful purchases she just received in the mail, accompanied by great pics or videos, she got online and gave *bad* reviews, and told them off for not having a box of any kind with their so-called "luxury items." You have to understand just how much of an influence we have after we receive your product. She could have made people want those items, but instead she didn't want to even advertise that she got them because she was so embarrassed by the presentation.

That is what brands must always keep in mind: we live in a public world today and nothing is off limits. There is no such thing as privacy or keeping things to yourself.

Remember the line "If you don't have anything nice to say, don't say anything at all"? Those days are gone! Everyone shares their thoughts and reactions, good or bad, and everyone wants to see them.

So when designing your packaging, you have to ask yourself, what are Gen-Zers going to see when your product gets to them? Are you going to impress us enough to share it? That is all that should be on your mind. Your entire business is being documented—and not just after the fact anymore, but in real time now as well, given all the live-streaming out there.

This is a huge trend that is not going away. Today, we all want the experience of shopping, purchasing, and receiving something that is *post-worthy and sharable.* So your research must begin with watching unpackaging videos and product reviews on YouTube. And don't forget the most important part: read the comments!

Another idea to consider is actually showing us what the packaging looks like ahead of time.

Post a video on your website showing real people receiving their online purchases. Potential customers *will* watch, and many will be drawn to buy just because they want not only the product but that experience of unpackaging. They want that box, that tissue paper—some kids just want the particular bubble wrap that comes with your packaging. I'm serious!

Another element of this is letting us peek at what our purchases will show up in so we know what we're waiting for. That makes the waiting more exciting.

You may not want us to know—you may want us to be surprised. But remember, there are good surprises and bad surprises. The difference today is, we record our surprises and post them for the world to see.

So make sure you've planned for this. Do you want a good reaction or a bad one? Do you want an excited customer or a disappointed one? Which one would you prefer to have reviewing you in front of dozens, hundreds, even thousands of potential customers? If a child receives your product and cries about the lack of packaging, do you want a video of that going viral? Because that is a definite possibility.

Finally, you have to consider potential collectors as part of your target audience.

For example, I collect rare, unused Ping golf balls. So I also have a Ping golf-ball box, which is highly desirable and collectible as well.

Recently I was approached by a serial entrepreneur to create custom luxury car-key boxes for luxury and supercar owners. He knew an entire market of luxury-car owners—a built-in clientele—who would want to place their high-end keys in a sophisticated box.

Do you think he was taking about a plain cardboard box? Or ordinary car keys?

No!

He wanted me to create an exceptional case that captured the attention of the luxury clientele who possess these magnificent keys that start these spectacular vehicles.

If you deliver your product in a plain, ordinary brown cardboard box, your brand will never be something to be desired or collected. We are creating a generation of new collectors. Give us something to collect!

Can We Get That Delivered?

Generation Zers want delivery everything! We're all about convenience and simplicity.

Do you know why Amazon is king (besides the fact that they don't empty your shopping cart)?

It's not because they offer the best prices—in fact they even change the prices of items in your cart. You'd think their customers would say, "What? How is this possible?" But instead Amazon gets away with it. Why?

Because consumers are still willing to make that purchase because it's *time efficient*. Especially to a Gen-Zer, time is the most important commodity. Gen-Zers don't want to go out for anything!

Delivery services are the future; I can't emphasize this enough. You must make *everything* delivery-friendly!

I didn't get paid to say Amazon is king. I just see that they are trying to break into every delivery/service market sector. They want you to come to them for everything. My father recently sent us an article mentioning Amazon and maid services in the same sentence. The article also said something like, "Imagine if Amazon figures out a way to ship alcohol around the country."

I'm sure they are working through those loopholes as I dictate this book.

Unlike many companies, Amazon works for most generations, and it will continue to work, especially for Generation Z, because of its simplicity of usage.

Since we even have Alexa in my house, all you have to do is tell her to order whatever it is for you. How much easier can this life get?

Here's an example of how much Gen-Zers need their ease of delivery.

Recently my brother texted my mom to tell her he'd had liquor delivered to his apartment in DC because it was raining and he was too lazy to go out! (Don't worry, he is over twenty-one).

My poor mother is still in shock! (First, because my brother can now legally purchase alcohol, and second, because she wasn't thrilled to hear liquor stores are now delivering.)

A more common version is that when Gen-Zers are sick they would rather pay Amazon for same-day delivery of Nyquil and Mucinex than walk to the pharmacy.

And forget all those urgent-care centers that are getting built on every corner. Gen-Zers aren't going.

In fact, we aren't thrilled with the online-doctor thing, either, as we want an in-person checkup. But we don't want to go to an urgent-care center; we are too busy. I understand that business-people think that urgent-care centers are about convenience, and that is probably true for all the older generations. They started this trend because a typical family doctor is only open nine to five Monday through Friday, so someone, probably some Baby Boomer, thought the idea of having doctors available after-hours and weekends, with no appointment necessary and hardly any wait, was the greatest thing since electricity.

I hate to break it to you, but this is *not* what Gen-Zers think of as the home run of convenience.

This is where the disconnect lies in understanding Generation Z. Something that other generations think is a great idea may not be for us.

You have to consider that times are changing. One of the biggest changes in terms of scheduling and availability is that a significant chunk of the workforce today works remotely, and this trend will only continue to rise.

They do not punch a time clock or have old-fashioned business hours. They work from home and they do it all the time, any time they can. There are no exact "business hours" anymore. My developer constantly emails me to let me know that she will be making fixes after she puts her little ones to bed at seven p.m.

So what may seem like convenient hours to one generation is no big deal to another.

The Gen-Zers who would rather order medicine than walk to the pharmacy? My brother is a perfect example. When he was sick my mother texted him to urge him to run over to the urgent-care center. He texted back his reasons for not going: he had a lot of studying to do, he had no time, he didn't know where one was, blah blah blah…

Within five seconds, my mother had Googled urgent-care facilities in DC's Tenleytown area, where my brother was staying, and there was literally one right next door to my brother's apartment building. My mother texted him the link.

She thought she was providing him with the "answer key."

But my brother replied, "No worries, I just ordered Mucinex and Tylenol from Amazon Same-Day Delivery."

I'm telling you, going to urgent care didn't rank high enough on my brother's list of priorities to use his valued time on. It was right next door, and he easily could have Googled it himself, but that's not what our generation considers convenient. He found another resource to meet his need. Same-day delivery of cold medicine is convenient, and convenience is the bottom line.

Now, if my mom could have sent a doctor over to him, sure. That would be convenient. Doctors simply need to start making house calls, like back in my mom's day. They could use Uber!

Every doctor should also be able to text the pharmacy the prescription; Gen-Zers will never take the time to drop off a physical script, let alone go back to pick it up. That would be a totally insane waste of time. And you can forget about a Gen-Zer ever waiting to have a prescription filled. That's never going to happen, not with this turned-on ADHD generation.

I know the big chain pharmacies are on the prescription-delivery wagon already, but what about your mom-and-pop pharmacies that are still hanging around? I know this will sound terrible, but we won't be loyal to them if they don't make prescriptions convenient. They will just become a thing of the past.

My mother tells me that only shut-ins had their prescriptions delivered back in the day. (The only time I'd heard the term "shut-in" was in a recent trailer for a scary movie by that name! Our generation had never heard that expression before the movie was released.) Well, we aren't shut-ins, but we know we want our scripts delivered.

The bottom line is, Gen-Zers will pay to not have to go out. Not just rich Gen-Zers, but Gen-Zers from all financial backgrounds. They will keep certain things high on their list of necessities, and will spend what it takes for what they feel is important to them. It's not for anyone else to judge what they spend their money on.

We have all witnessed the convenience of Uber, Lyft, GrubHub, Caviar, and the many other meal- and grocery-delivery services. The success of these services is an indicator of where we're headed.

Simply put, delivery is a necessity to us, not a luxury, and if your company isn't on that delivery wagon, we will find one that is.

No-Interaction Car-Buying/Leasing

GEN-ZERS WANT TO BUY OR lease our cars online. We don't want to call anyone or talk to them in person. We don't want any hidden fees or charges.

We want honesty; don't try anything shady. We want to see the exact prices up front—no sneaking in a hidden return fee, accidentally forgetting to tell us about extra charges, adding taxes after the fact, etc. We not only will go elsewhere but will also write a scathing review.

What's more, we want it done in seven minutes, and we want the car delivered!

We don't care if it's a Mercedes or a Kia. We will sign all paperwork very quickly in person or electronically, via scan or email. We like our autonomy and see no reason to go to the dealership for hours of negotiation.

If we want to test drive a model, we will go to the dealership, but that doesn't necessarily mean we want to sit and talk to salesmen and negotiate.

For that matter, if you do see us looking at cars in your lot, the fewer questions you ask us the better. If we are interested in a car, *we* will contact you. Gen-Zers don't like to be needlessly bothered; we'll walk away. And when we do want your attention, we want it from the top person. We don't have time to waste on nobodies; we only want to deal with people who can make decisions.

We aren't doing a ton of back and forth. We know what we want and have already researched the correct prices. We are educated and informed and are not interested in someone trying to rip us off.

How to Make YouTube Work for You

"The single most important strategy in content marketing today is video."
— Gary Vaynerchuk, serial entrepreneur, speaker,
New York Times bestselling author

YOUTUBE HAS OVER ONE BILLION users, which is almost an entire third of all the people on the Internet. According to StatisticBrain.com, three hundred hours of video is uploaded to YouTube every minute, and nearly five billion videos are viewed each day.

Do you understand numbers like that? No other network has those kinds of stats.

One thing this means is that there is endless content for us to watch without ever having to see a rerun! According to YouTube's statistics, it reaches more Gen-Zers and Millennials than any cable network in America.

So this is where marketers want to be. But since they are up against over a billion users, all fighting for exposure, it is hard for marketers to break into that space.

That is where influence marketing comes in big time.

You must start to use the YouTubers that Gen-Zers know and watch as your marketing influencers. You must recognize them as your tool for advertising.

No, they are not the conventional influencers, but they *are* our generation's influencers, and we are your target market. Gen-Zers talk about their influencers as if they're our friends. Their Instagram stories and live-streaming are connecting us to their lives.

I can tell you: Multiple times a day, I click on a YouTube video and first have to wait the five to fourteen long seconds for the commercial to end to hit the "skip ad" button. During this painful waiting period, I would *much* rather be watching Roman Atwood doing a car commercial, for example, than having to sit through some nobody I don't even recognize doing it. Let him do it his way, the way we like to watch our TV today, and we will probably not hate the advertisements so much.

Most companies have zero idea of the power of influencers in today's world—probably because they don't watch YouTube. That shouldn't matter; what matters is that your target market does.

Just because you don't understand a space doesn't mean you shouldn't be there. Rather, you should admit it and seek the help and expertise of someone who does.

You can't be an expert in every area of your business. That is why you hire professionals: to help with what you don't know. Hire for your weaknesses.

Here's an example of an influencer.

I started my luxury-car-review website, SkysCars.com, when I was nine years old. I didn't start my YouTube channel until last year, when I was eleven.

I have visited and videoed at more luxury- and exotic-car dealerships around the world than most people ever will. I have never used any marketing for either my YouTube channel or my website.

Yet I have five thousand YouTube subscribers, and millions of views on my videos. (I know that in the big YouTube picture those numbers are not huge—but I'm just a kid, I'm nobody. I'm not marketing anything; I'm just having fun.)

On the other hand, take a look at the YouTube channels of the multi-million-dollar luxury- and exotic-car dealerships I've made those videos at. I can tell you, I, as a kid, have more subscribers and hits on my simple SkysCars YouTube channel than most of them. Probably not what they're aiming for!

These top luxury- and exotic-car dealerships have huge marketing/advertising budgets. They have whole teams of people promoting campaigns for their supercars.

Yet they only have fifty to a hundred and fifty YouTube subscribers. Some of the dealerships have literally three videos from six years ago on these magnificent vehicles, each with just a hundred and thirty views, maybe up to five thousand views.

Who wouldn't want to watch a video of the majestic Rolls-Royce Phantom? I have no problem getting nine hundred thousand views on a car half as nice.

No one would believe that these multi-million-dollar companies just let that end of social media slide. But they simply don't take advantage of influencers. Do you know how many dealers linked to my videos—you know, the ones with millions of hits promoting their own cars in their own showrooms?

Not one!

No one ever linked my videos to their site or YouTube channel. I get hundreds of thousands of hits on those videos; it was literally free advertising for their products and their dealerships.

What an opportunity—not one of these expensive teams of marketing and social media experts ever thought to link to me. They all loved me, and they loved my videos, and the best part was I used to work for free! Yet they never asked me if they could link to me. My father used to marvel at how every time we left a dealership, the top people would say, "Omg, I love your videos, I watch your YouTube channel, come back and make more!"

In the car afterward, my dad would exclaim to my mom and me, "Are these people crazy? Why don't they ask to link to Sky; it's free advertising he's doing for them! Why would anyone turn that down?"

It's not that they turned it down. They just didn't think of it.

They don't have the open-minded marketing people, or anyone who specializes in social media marketing, that they need to see the power an influencer can have, even if the influencer is a nine-year-old kid.

They don't see my videos as being an outlet or promotional tool for them. These are old-school, hands-on owners who just aren't thinking of how to futurize their private companies.

It gets worse—some of them *do* try to bring their companies into the future and fail at it. Some dealers started making their own videos of these supercars…but featuring strange, awkward salesmen that no one wants to watch. These are the videos they use on their YouTube channels, which could be such a huge promotional outlet for them. Sometimes they try to make them with hot girls, and that helps to get a pinch more views, but nothing compared to my viewership or the hits other, much larger YouTube influencers get—influencers who could be making different videos for these top dealerships.

Pictures and videos are the most powerful tools in our generation's arsenal. We use the heck out of them. Businesses should care about taking the right steps in order to be viewed in the best light.

Gen-Zers have more influential power than the news actually writes about. When a kid like me at eleven years old has one million hits on one of his YouTube videos with *zero* advertising, shouldn't that tell you something? Lots of us, in our own ways, are little superstars!

Wouldn't you like to have a million visitors? Some companies/brands never see numbers like that. And some see a ton more than that. But most are still behind the times with video.

They really have no concept of just how much time Generation Z spends watching videos. Videos about anything and everything. Gen-Zers don't want to read content; they want to watch it. That is why the video length Instagram allows you to upload recently went from fifteen seconds to sixty seconds, and why they now offer live-streaming, along with every other social media platform.

So video marketing should be where most of your budget is spent. Even if it's just on your website or blog, make videos instead of all written content. No matter what industry you are in, from hospitality to luxury products to fashion. There is nothing that can't be captured in a video.

YouTube is not even close to realizing its potential. You can recruit the most influential stars: YouTubers, Generation Z's celebrities.

Companies simply haven't realized that a nobody from nowhere can get millions of subscribers and followers watching their videos, usually with small budgets, because they are high in creativity. These YouTube stars are able to grab the six-second attention span of Gen-Zers to keep them watching a twenty-five-minute video. That's a pretty impressive accomplishment. So why wouldn't you think they are good enough to make a lousy sixty-second commercial for your brand?

Not that I don't enjoy seeing LeBron and other top athletes, stars, and models representing brands and companies, but you have the opportunity to really grab our attention and maybe even loyalty by using the people we actually spend time with on YouTube. (Not to mention you can pay them a ton less money as well, because we all know how much you spend on top athletes and superstars.)

I understand there have been issues with YouTubers not being politically correct and getting in trouble and causing controversy in the news. So companies and brands will say they are afraid to use them, for fear of them straying from representing their brand in a good light.

But the fact is, there are plenty of top athletes and celebrities who have strayed from being the most idol-like representation of brands. The bottom line is, we don't know who we can trust to represent a brand for any length of time, as this world is entirely public, and therefore there is nowhere to hide their screw-ups. But remember, the screw-ups are also what make us human. Everyone, to a certain degree, deserves a second chance…if it weren't for second chances, we would never know the Iron Man (Robert Downey Jr.) we all love and respect.

One of the mistakes brands/companies are making today is failing to notice or celebrate anyone else's strengths. Only the top stars and athletes in the country get endorsements. Are they real and relatable people? No!

Brands like Nike and Under Amour only give endorsements to the very top kid athletes—how many kids can relate to them? Most kids today aren't even athletic!

On the flip side, how many kids can relate to a YouTube kid (or even adult—just any real person on YouTube) creating tons of entertaining content that we stream daily? We all can. Those people are creating connections with us. We can relate to them when they are being represented by a larger brand.

You need to give these stars of our time creative freedom.

It's like when a professional painter comes over to paint the interior of my house. They show my mom a thousand colors and ask her to choose. My mother always says, "You are the artist. I want you to have creative freedom as to what you think will look best on these walls with these furnishings and fabrics."

The artist is always thrilled to hear this.

Brands should be open to hearing the creative genius these self-made stars bring to the table. If they are able to create content that engages millions of viewers, I think it's worth hearing their input about how to engage customers for your brand.

I don't think the older generations have respect for YouTube talent, or consider it real talent yet. But just because you can't understand it doesn't mean it doesn't exist. If you don't get it, then hire open-minded people or younger demographics to deal with marketing to this generation. You are killing your companies by staying behind the times.

Here's a great recent example. In the winter of 2016 a toy called Hatchimals came out. Here's a company who did some things right and some things wrong.

First, they were inspired to create Hatchimals because they noticed the major popularity of YouTube unpackaging videos, and they wanted to design a toy that mimicked that. They paid attention to what this generation likes, and it paid off.

Second, they marketed this toy to young girls. Remember when I said this generation doesn't care about gender-specific marketing? Well, Hatchimals became popular with girls *and* boys, young and older.

Finally, they only made twenty-five thousand Hatchimals for the entire Christmas season. Then they sent one to some top YouTube kid, who made a video of how a Hatchimal works. Guess how many views it got? Ten million. Guess what happened next? Every child needed to have one, and parents ended up desperately paying $500 each for a $50 toy at the last second.

Not from a commercial at all. All from a YouTube video.

How to Make Instagram Work for You

"Marketing is no longer about the stuff that you make, but about the stories that you tell."
— Seth Godin, entrepreneur, marketer, best-selling author

SURPRISINGLY, TONS OF BUSINESSES AND companies do not practice good Instagram business strategy.

Often, the person in their company who handles their social media accounts has zero marketing or advertising experience. Now, just because someone knows how to set up a social media account (which a seven-year-old can do) does not mean they know how to use it as a business tool.

That is one of the biggest mistakes I see happening in companies today. They throw some techie or web-designer or even amateur blogger the task of setting up all the social media accounts for the company and make them responsible for keeping them updated.

But this is not the person who should be handling your social media posts. You need a top marketing professional. Not just any marketer; they must be a social media specialist, or else they are just wasting your time and money with ineffective posts. You need to keep this in line with your brand-marketing budget.

Generation Z doesn't look at magazines, newspapers, or anything in print form, so you must move at least 80% of your advertising to mobile. Consider Instagram, YouTube, and even Snapchat the most valuable tools in your box.

Today, nearly all teenagers and young adults use social media. Social media has rapidly grown into the key tool to reach the Gen Z market.

Recently, Instagram posted that it officially reached seven hundred million users. The fact that we are a following generation means that anyone can be an influencer today. This could be a great thing for businesses.

But keep in mind: seven hundred million users are not just followers but *unfollowers* as well!

Over eighty million photos and videos are uploaded to Instagram per day.

But businesses/brands should not just be focused on uploading a pic. Instagram isn't just based on uploading a photo—that's what Pinterest is for. Generation Z sees the commercial side of Instagram very differently than they see the personal Instagram posts of their friends and families.

So to use Instagram effectively as a business/brand, you have to know what your goal is. Ask yourself:

- Why does my business need Instagram?
- What are we trying to say with the pic or video we post?
- Are we trying to get people to our website? Are we trying to launch a product or business? Are we trying to sell existing

products to a new audience? Are we trying to gain exposure for a promotional deal?

Let me give you the facts about what Gen-Zers actually want to see in a commercial post.

If the product is something you can take a video of, then don't just show us a pic; show us a video "series" of how we can use it. These videos should address all the questions we'll have about the product. For example, let's say you're selling a drone. *Show* us examples that answer the questions we'll have about it. And don't put all the product info in one post—tell us in pieces to keep us "following" you. Isn't that the point of Instagram? If you're not using it that way, you need to be. It's one of your greatest advertising and marketing tools.

You need to use it as an ongoing advertising campaign, like back in the day. For our example drone, this could look like:

First post, show us a short peek video (or even a picture).

Next: maybe a short video of it being used, in just one scenario.

Next: different color options or models.

Do you see what I'm doing?

I'm building your followers' anticipation...

You still haven't posted when it's coming out or where you can buy it. By this point people are sharing your posts and tagging each other in your comments; they are building your following for you.

For the next few posts, offer videos of different ways the drone could be used. For example, inside, outside, on the beach, over the water, on a mountain. Show it being used by different genders and age groups. Remember that your marketing demographics today are much larger than you think. It's not a boy/girl world anymore.

Make sure you are using relevant #hashtags, but not too many of them. Two hashtags is actually the magic number. People may tell you differently, but you get more interactions with two #hashtags than with ten. If you don't believe me, look at Nike #hashtags: never more than two. It doesn't matter that they are Nike—it's finding the one relevant word that will get you interactions.

Also keep in mind that these videos should address the questions we'll have about the drone's usage: What are its limitations? Where do you suggest we use the drone? What's the level of difficulty for using it? Is it durable or easily breakable? (Be honest.)

Then, when the product is going to be in stores and/or available for purchase online, it's time to tell us all the places we can get it from and to reveal the cost.

There is really nothing more frustrating than seeing a pic or watching a video on Instagram and not being able to find what product it is or where to purchase it. And this is a very common problem.

If you are a brand that actually produces a physical product, for example, Old Gringo boots, you can make videos of the product being made—let's say a specific style of boot. We love to watch videos, and will especially appreciate the craftsmanship aspect of your product if you give us insight into it. Bonus: it will also justify the high price of the product when we see an artist creating this work of arts.

It could be candy being made, Murano glass being blown, an artist painting, a sculptor creating—anything made by hand. Show us how the process works. We are visual creatures today.

Gen-Zers are like sponges. We will remember the video, talk about it, and share it to social media platforms as well. Involve us and we become advertising for you!

Another useful strategy is involving YouTube in this process. Once you've started offering these craftsmanship videos, start placing different or more in-depth versions along the same lines up on YouTube. The more visibility you give these videos, the more we will watch and share them.

Nike is ranked in the top twenty most-followed Instagram accounts for a reason. If you haven't noticed, nine out of every ten of their Instagram posts are now in video form. They know how to engage us.

They also tell you the exact product name in the post so you can actually go and buy it. They get how to use the tool.

Companies that make or sell jewelry in particular need to hop on this train. When it comes to Instagram campaigns (or even just website ads) for jewelry brands, you must show not only the piece you have for sale but also a pic of someone wearing it. I see custom-jewelry designers making this mistake all the time.

We need to see how the piece looks on the wrist/finger/neck/ear, etc. I often see something like a funky-shaped bracelet with comments from viewers asking, "Can you show me a pic of this being worn? Can't really picture how it fits."

If you want people to buy your jewelry, show multiple angles of someone wearing it, or even a short video of someone putting it on. This especially applies to bracelets—most viewers wonder—and ask in the comments—whether you need to have a tiny hand to get it on or if a bigger hand can fit through it.

Your customers are telling you what they want—listen to them!

Instagram is an advertising vehicle. Make sure you have the right people driving!

Tell Us the Details

Do you know why pictures are set up to be spreadable on our mobile devices?

Because we are nosy.

We want to see not only the main point of the pic or video but also every single solitary thing in the entire picture—background, sides, top to bottom, and every space in between.

Do you realize that is why Instagram added zoom to their platform? They know how nosy our society is today, and that we're getting more inquisitive every day.

That's why when I post a pic or video, I try my best to add the all the details: the name and style of my sneakers, the location and name of the restaurant I'm eating at, the amazing dessert on my plate. Whatever is within eyesight and zoom sight will be seen by your followers, and they will want to know information about everything visible in that pic.

Hashtags and Captions

COMPANIES CONSTANTLY POST TO INSTAGRAM with stupid hashtags that have nothing to do with the pic they are actually posting.

This is fine for personal Instagram accounts, when you want to show little Bobby rolling his first bowling ball and say #strike #bestballer, etc.

But I'm talking about brands with thousands of followers, even tens of thousands of followers. It is sad to see home goods, clothing, and accessories sites posting amazing high-end furniture, fashions, handbags, jewelry, and everything you can think of without bothering to write descriptive captions telling you what products are actually in these pics and videos they are uploading.

Fantasy Stock

When is someone going to establish that Instagram is not *only* about the quality of the picture? We care about the picture communicating actual, usable information, and about the caption having high-quality content (information) as well.

Why are businesses posting pics of items that aren't in stock, or sometimes not even in their inventory at all?

Don't their advertising teams understand the point of using social media? The point is to get people to look at your post and decide to come to your site to purchase the item. It's not that difficult to comprehend. Yet they are all messing up.

Go see for yourself. Their viewers' comments tell the whole story. They're begging for info.

For example, a business posts a pic of a pair of boots. All the comments say variations of "Where can I buy those boots??" The business posts a pic of a girl wearing a sports bra and workout pants on the beach. The comments say, "Plz share where that sports bra is from!"

No reply to those comments…because they don't sell the boots, or the sports bra.

People are asking, "Where can I buy that bag? Where do I get this table? How do I find this rug? Where are the shoes from? Who sells that gray nightstand and that leopard pillow? I want to buy that headboard, but where? How do I buy this bracelet?" They are literally begging you to sell things to them, and you're ignoring them.

These commenters are telling the truth. They often say, "I want and need everything on here." Yet there is zero information regarding how or where to buy these products, as if they don't exist.

These companies are completely missing out on Instagram's potential as a marketing tool. They're trying to sell potential customers on an experience or an idea, but instead they're turning them off by posting fantasy pics—pics of items they don't even offer. That is what Pinterest is for.

Why waste your followers' attention? And how about if every once in a while you actually have your social media handlers reply to these comments?

It's not just frustrating that you don't tell us how to get our hands on those items. It actually turns us away, because we know you don't carry those items and are baiting us with fantasy pictures. That's like showing people pictures of castles when you only sell sheds!

All of the above goes for posts from brick-and-mortar stores too. Why post a pic if you aren't going to tell us where we can buy the products shown in it?

If I work for a funky custom-golf-cart business, for example, and I post a pic of a golf cart, you can bet I'm putting the exact make, model, and color, along with the link to buy.

Airbnb is a good example of poor Instagram content strategy. They have tons of photos of destinations, taken by both professional photographers and regular tourists/travelers. Now, any given photo will be featured on the Instagram feeds of both Airbnb and the professional photographer, but neither will offer much or any information regarding the actual photo you're looking at. Simply tagging the photo with "Harihari, New Zealand," or just the photographer's name, doesn't help us at all!

Do you think we are going to go to the actual website and search all Harihari, New Zealand, listings to find that pic? That is not what Gen-Zers expect from a social media post. We want to know the exact location of the picture.

Remember, we want one-stop shopping. Gen-Zers want a seamless transition from the Instagram post to the product/location/experience/food, whatever it may be. We are willing to click on one or two links at most to find that answer.

For example, we often see something like a magnificent pic of an outdoor bathtub in some enchanted forest with no information included. We would appreciate if you told us what season we could take that outdoor bath in—not to mention where this bathtub is actually located. Does it even exist, or is it a photoshopped or fantasy picture, like the ones on Pinterest?

Gen-Zers are not interested in fake marketing, and we're really not going to put any time or effort into searching further to find out more about this bathtub.

Maybe that was a Millennial thing, but it is certainly not a Gen Z thing. We don't have time for that; we will just move on.

You are wasting social media hits with these dead ends. You are supposed to post what you have, not stuff you think we want to see pictures of. Why would we keep following you if you can't connect us to the product to purchase? And why would we ever use our influence in a positive way for you—do you think I'm going to send my friend a pic of something I think he might like while knowing your post is informationless?

What is the method to your social media madness?

Like I have said regarding every sector: if you are posting a pic to any social media outlet, you must include where to purchase every detail, down to the nail polish the model is wearing.

People will zoom in to see what's in the pic. It is actually easier than ever to see things. But you have to tell us the product names and where to buy them.

If you do not have the product, or, at the very least, info on the products, do NOT post the pic! It is such a tease and turn off to us.

Here's what happens if you don't follow this advice:

We stop following you, and start following someone else.

It really is as easy as that. That's right: if you can't fulfill our needs and are only baiting us with nice pics of things you don't actually carry, we will not only stop following you, meaning you lose a whole generation of customers, but also go find somewhere that actually does carry products like that—meaning your competitors just beat you.

Articles say Generation Z has no brand loyalty. Well, we also have no social media loyalty, especially if you lie to us or mislead us. That is not what Gen-Zers want to be wasting their time on. End of story.

What's Your Cause?

Gen-Zers are informed and caring. Our generation wants to make a difference, to give back, and to know that our purchases aren't just for ourselves—they need to be helping others in some way.

I give back by letting Gen-Zers share their strengths on my GenZInsider.com platform, as that is my "thing," my passion.

So companies/businesses/brands need to be into philanthropy! Let Gen-Zers know you care about a cause. Tell us what your passion is, give to a related cause, and tell us why you give to that cause. Maybe the founder's mother died of cancer so the company gives to the Susan G. Komen fund. Maybe the owner loves her rescue dog so the business gives to the ASPCA. Tell us!

It will make you real and relatable, and will let us know that you aren't only getting rich off of our purchase. We need to know that you are paying it forward to something that touches your heart. And it will touch us as well.

That is why TOMS does so well—everyone knows the "one for one" campaign, where they give a free pair of shoes to someone in need when you make a purchase. This way, instead of feeling guilty about a purchase, we feel great about it because we know we are somehow contributing to helping others.

Now TOMS has added more charitable practices beyond "one for one." They know that it works to draw customers *and* it does concrete good in the world—a win-win for both company and customer.

Hiring in the Digital Age

"Here's to the crazy ones. The misfits. The rebels. The troublemakers. The round pegs in the square holes. The ones who see things differently. They're not fond of rules. And they have no respect for the status quo. You can quote them, disagree with them, glorify or vilify them. About the only thing you can't do is ignore them. Because they change things. They push the human race forward. And while some may see them as the crazy ones, we see genius. Because the people who are crazy enough to think they can change the world, are the ones who do."
— from Apple's "Think Different" campaign by Rob Siltanen, creative director

IT IS TIME TO START drafting your Gen Z team.

This may be the most important team you ever put together. This team may mean the difference between the survival of your company, or its extinction. No pressure...lol.

I can't end this book until I give you the real Answer Key. I will be completely honest with you, and I hope you listen and truly hear everything I'm about to tell you.

My second-largest strength in my dyslexic arsenal is the ability to recognize the strengths in others.

I attend a school for kids who learn differently, which means we can't learn in the conventional manner most of the world does. We compensate for our weaknesses on a daily basis. We use our strengths to guide us. Some of these kids keep to themselves, and not all have the best social skills. They are the ones who probably don't make eye contact or even shake hands.

But they are the ones who are digital/tech geniuses. They are the ones who probably sat alone at the school lunch table, and as adults in the office they are probably the ones who wear the hoodies and keep their headphones on. They are the ones whose names you probably don't know. They are probably not the ones you are grabbing a drink or playing ball with after work. More than likely, they are the ones who never look up from their computer screens, who stay in their cubicles all day.

Or even the opposite—they may have been the kids playing video games while pacing around the room, and now as adults in the office they are the ones with the standing desks. The ones who don't shut up and have a million things to share. The ones who constantly talk about video games or technology. The ones who go to Comic-Con.

These are probably the greatest minds of our time.

Here's my advice: I urge companies to be more open-minded than ever before.

You must be ready to embrace differences. I'm not talking about the nose-ring or gauged-ear or tattoo kind of different.

I'm talking about the different thinkers. The ones whose answers are anything but what you expect them to be.

But the only way these different thinkers are going to have a chance at being drafted to your team is if you do not do things the old-fashioned way.

Because just like I cannot learn at a regular school, these different thinkers cannot go through the regular channels of the hiring process. They cannot be interviewed by your behind-the-times "human resources manager."

That should not be the person drafting the most important team of your life. They do not have the eye to spot these different thinkers, and are not trained to identify with them.

My mom is like the Dyslexia/ADHD/Autism Spectrum Whisperer. She gets all of us. She can read dyslexic, and she edits the dyslexic articles for my website. She sees how gifted different thinkers are, just like I do. We see their differences as the most interesting part of them. They make you laugh, they say things that are off the wall, and they can come up with ideas you never dreamed of. This is their strength.

They may not have the best people skills, or they may over-compensate for their lack of people skills. You may not be able to relate to them in any way or any conversation. They may be what you consider "nerds" or "strange" or "weird." They may be dyslexic, have ADHD, be on the autism spectrum, have OCD. They may have issues you haven't even heard of. They may tell you about their issues, or they may not. But these are the ones you want on your team! These are the smart kids. I'm talking krazy smart. They may even spell it with a *K* like me; who cares?

When these different thinkers submit an application, it may look strange and over the top, or completely insane. So you're going to need someone in your company who can identify these different thinkers on paper, as well as in person. They're probably not going to be the ones who can pass the personality part of their interview. They may not pass the manners test, the political-correctness test, the having-a-filter test, and the other social tests an HR manager is going to throw at them. So you need someone who can recognize their strengths and potential.

You must be ready to embrace these different thinkers, because they are the future.

Now, it's not new that they are our brilliant minds. They always have been. However, traditionally it's been hard for these different thinkers to land the top careers, because they can't get past the recruiters, with their old way of thinking, and the HR managers, with their clueless eyes and stuffy tests.

How will you get these top thinkers on your team if you don't change your in-house rules? Not all of these great-minded people can be expected to become entrepreneurs simply because that's their only means of having a shot at employment. They deserve a shot at a career they can absolutely excel in. They just need to get past the front door.

Please try not to judge. Don't let the HR department pick apart these applicants. These applicants are my friends, and I see how incredibly brilliant they are. They are the most interesting, hilarious, and brilliant people, the least boring players you could ever have on your team.

If you give them a hand (not literally, because some of them don't like to be touched), I promise you won't be disappointed.

They will give you 150%. Being in business, you should recognize that that's a pretty profitable number.

www.ingramcontent.com/pod-product-compliance
Lightning Source LLC
Chambersburg PA
CBHW060858170526
45158CB00001B/410